S0-AWU-283

The
No-Garden Gardener:

Container Gardening

on Balconies, Decks,

Patios and Porches

The
No-Garden Gardener:

Container Gardening
on Balconies, Decks,
Patios and Porches

Edwinna von Baeyer

and

Dinah Shields

Random House
Toronto, New York, London, Sydney, Auckland

Copyright © 1993 by Edwinna von Baeyer
and Dinah Shields

All rights reserved under International and Pan-American
Copyright Conventions.

Published in Canada in 1993 by Random House of Canada
Limited, Toronto.

Canadian Cataloguing in Publication Data

von Baeyer, Edwinna, 1947-
   The no-garden gardener : container gardening on
balconies, decks, patios and porches

ISBN 0-394-22338-1

I. Container gardening. I. Shields, Dinah.
II. Title.

SB418.V65 1993   635.9'86   C93-093288-9

Design and illustrations: Teri McMahon
Printed and bound in Canada
10 9 8 7 6 5 4 3 2 1

DEDICATION

To Gisela Sommer, the container gardener par excellence!
EvB

For Miguel, who was such a nice surprise.
DJS

CONTENTS

Do you define a garden as a vast, rolling lawn edged by
voluptuous flowerbeds but only have a deck, balcony, porch
or patio to work with? Renting a house or "garden home"
and don't want to invest in permanent plantings that will
have to be left behind? Stuck in a balcony with green thumbs
twitching? Have only a postage-stamp sized deck or patio
and no soil in sight? Do not despair. There is another way to
garden — in a pot, up a trellis, in a hanging basket or a
window box. These are just a few of the ways to achieve
maximum horticultural impact in a minimum of space.

Housing lots are becoming smaller and smaller all the
time, as municipalities squish ten houses into a space that,
twenty years ago, would have held six. Unfortunately, this
doesn't leave much space for the gardeners who want to act
out their Kew Gardens and Versailles fantasies.

We hope our book will tell you all you need to know to
design and maintain big ideas in a small space. Even a small
balcony can become that tranquil oasis you've always
wanted, the one that takes you away from the bustle of
everyday life. Gardening in confined spaces has its own set
of challenges, but we think that a challenge can be seen as an
opportunity, too.

We wish to thank our editor Anna Cundari for seeing us
through another book — calmly and enthusiastically.
(Thanks also to Anna's mum for coming up with the idea in
the first place.) Shaun Oakey did a great job finding

inconsistencies and muddy meanings and, in general, clearing the decks, so to speak. Edwinna wishes to thank her family for enduring yet another book deadline with humor and patience. Dinah would like to thank Cheryl and Michelle Kennedy for friendship and welcome distraction from the computer screen.

Although we were helped through this particular garden by editors and family and friends, any errors are due only to us.

Edwinna von Baeyer

Dinah Shields

Ottawa, 1993

Chapter 1

Amazing Space:

Designing the Container Garden

....
Many people who have only a small area to garden in look at it with a sigh and a feeling that they are getting second best — "best" being a big lawn edged with lots of densely planted flowerbeds and shaded by a collection of massive trees. To which we say phooey. Life is too short to waste time longing for what you don't have. Think instead of the benefits of a small-scale container garden created within the confines of a deck, patio, porch or balcony:

- no grass to mow,
- no grass edges to maintain around in-ground flowerbeds,
- less weeding, since there is air, not earth, between potted plants,

- easier weeding, because you are not down on your hands and knees at ground level,
- less water consumption, since water is poured into a collection of pots, not over flowerbeds and lawn,
- easier customizing of growing conditions for finicky pot plants than in ordinary flowerbeds,
- easier rearrangement if you are not happy with the design or effect,
- creativity — pots, furniture and plants can change position and variety every year,
- none of the back-breaking labor necessary when growing perennial plants, because you will be growing annuals almost exclusively (Why? See Appendix I),
- just enough absorbing little jobs to do: a few minutes here picking off bugs, a few there weeding, a few more watering — pleasant ways to spend some idle summer time,
- and remember, no grass to mow.

DESIGN WITHOUT TEARS

Design First, Plant Later is our firmly held motto, since we both have learned the hard way what happens when you do not.

We have been gardening for a long time, but we must confess that the "D" word still alarms and intimidates us. It comforted us to realize that creating an outdoor room can be broken down into just three steps.

First, take a long, hard look at what you have to work

with. The most important part of this step is thinking about your personality, your likes and dislikes, and your practical needs. This includes an estimate of how much plant maintenance you have the time and temperament for. As well, it includes seeing what is commercially available in the way of pots, furniture, plants, and so on.

The second step is to evaluate what you learned in the first step and let it guide your design decisions. Drawing up an actual design plan will help. We hope the cut-outs in Appendix II will be a further help with this. We hope, too, that you will make several different plans over a period of time, letting your ideas mellow and change, not rushing into things you will regret afterwards. (Anybody interested in buying a large wooden gate, unused, going cheap?)

The third is to do it. (Yippee — time to go shopping!)

Getting to Know Yourself

When we asked a professional furniture designer how to sneak up on the design process so that it was less frightening, he said, "Think first about function." This cheered us up considerably, since it enabled us to fit the exalted notion of designing things into the real world, the one we inhabit every day.

Thus you can design your outdoor space on the basis of the answers to a few practical questions. The answers will guide your decisions on what to buy and how to arrange it. Once these practical decisions have been made, you will be startled by how easily the artistic side of things falls into place. Here are some points to consider:

Making the Most of It

Everyone says, "I want to make the most of the small space I've got." This is an excellent principle, except that it means different things to different people. Does it mean you want to cram in as many interesting plants and objects as possible? Or do you want to make it look as big and spacious as possible? Either way is fine, but you will have to make up your mind — if you cannot, you can decide that you are in the middle, as we are. We do acknowledge the people who are crammers but who will take it to extremes. They will create a dizzyingly delightful garden that is a riotous mass of mingled greenery, flowers, statuary, whirligigs, and furniture. They will follow no one's rules, so we make none for them. Except the rules of plant maintenance — no one gets around those.

Crammers

Are you a crammer? You will want to inject a small degree of unity and connectedness into your space, since clutter, however charming, looks better for being a little organized. There should be room for people to walk safely through the space, or else no one will be able to admire it to the extent it deserves. Choice items in the crammer's repertoire are plant stands, trellises, and hanging baskets. (For more information about containers and their accessories, see Chapters 3 and 4.)

Spacious Living

Are you spaciously inclined? Then your basic goal is to

make a small space look bigger. The key to achieving this is to use a minimum of planters and furniture, all in the same style. Remember, each object you choose will have a big effect in a small space — mistakes really stand out. Keep a clear central floor space with everything at the edges.

Middle-Grounders

Are you a middle-grounder? If so, you can have the best of both worlds — a goodly mass of plants, just enough furniture, plus reasonable space for people to circulate through. The key lies in following the Golden Mean — not going overboard in either direction.

Under Surveillance

What are you going to do in your space? Entertain? Read? Eat? Sleep? Sunbathe? Hide out from the heat? Watch the rain come down? Observe your family and yourself in your outdoor room for two or three weeks, noting what everyone does, and then apply what you find out to your design decisions.

Formal?

Do you want a formally designed space? This will influence the style of furniture you buy and what it is made of — plastic furniture may be out and wrought iron or cast aluminum may be in. Choose classically designed containers made of stone or terra cotta, rather than unfinished, weathered cedar. Color schemes are more restrained —

whites and pale blues, perhaps, instead of reds and oranges. Homely items, such as a gas barbecue, can be screened from view with greenery or latticework. There is a lot of symmetry in a formal layout.

Informal?

Do you want an informally designed space? Symmetry is out the window. Materials are rougher and less refined — cast aluminum is out, molded plastics and heavy wood pieces are in. The gas barbecue sits where it is used, with little or no attempt at disguise. Color schemes are more exuberant — blues, pinks and yellows, or reds, blues and oranges.

Live to Party?

Do you entertain a lot? Lots of level, clear surfaces are important. Buy extra chairs and a second, fold-away dining table to be brought out for special parties. Can you arrange a little dance floor? Nothing nicer than dancing under the stars (but keep the music down, to be fair to the neighbors). Stick to narrow planters placed close to walls and railings so they do not take space away from circulation and dining areas. Avoid round or square containers, which might protrude into traffic paths.

Traffic

Observe the natural traffic flow and use it to show off the space's best features. Do people congregate along the railing to admire the sunset? Position a line of potted plants so people are directed towards it. Or hide it a little, so that those finding it can enjoy the sensation of having discovered a secluded treasure.

Head 'Em Up, Move 'Em Out

You can manipulate traffic flow to move people away from crowded areas. For example, whether you are barbecuing for twenty guests or just serving your family, carefully plan the refreshments area. People should find it, take what they want and leave to make room for others. Ensure this by setting tall potted plants in a row about 24 in./60 cm in front of the refreshments table. This leaves just enough room for people loading up to pass easily, but is narrow enough to encourage them to move away once their glasses and plates are full.

Custom-Made

If only a small number of people, say, just family members, will ever use the space, you can cater to everyone's likes. Two big loungers for sunbathers. A big bulky Adirondack (or Muskoka) chair for readers. A sun-shading umbrella for the fair-skinned.

Kiddy Time

Will children use the space? Please read Chapter 16 on general safety, especially if your outdoor garden is above ground level. Make sure children have an area where they can make a mess and no one will hound them about it — it's only fair, they live there too. A small table and kid-sized chairs might please them. Teenagers? The only thing that pleases them is if you vacate the space entirely.

After Dark

Will you use the space in the daytime or evening? To encourage more evening use, plan your plant selections accordingly: many flowers smell stronger after dark, and white flowers are much more visible after dusk. And take a close look at our section on lighting in this chapter.

Gimme Shelter

Want shelter from the rain or sun? Would an awning or roofed gazebo make sense? Either one is lovely, but remember that only low-light plants can be grown in such shady locations.

Work, Work, Work,
That's All I Do Around Here

How much time can you realistically devote to maintenance? A big mistake many of us make is to cram a small space with too many features, plants and furnishings, then find we do not have the time or temperament to keep it all in good order. If you find you have planted more than you want to maintain, consider giving the excess away to friends and neighbors. No point in grimly soldiering on and making yourself cranky. On the other hand, if time is not a factor, watering, bug-picking and weeding can be absorbing, relaxing and rewarding outdoor activities. And it all counts as exercise.

The Budgetary-Reality Crowd

What is your budget? Sure, it's nice to spend $25,000 on an outdoor remodel with a hot tub and custom-fitted stone planters and a fantastic lighting system, but not realistic for most of us. Resign yourself and choose affordable details such as inexpensive but nicely shaped molded plastic furniture or two strategically placed half-barrels. And remember that most annuals cost about the same amount, so your plants will cost just the same as those used in the fanciest gardens in town.

The Gold-Tap-for-the-Hose Crowd

Can you afford an extensive remodeling job? Instead of asking a contractor to do the work, consider having it done by a garden designer. The cost is not that much different, and a professional designer comes up with amazing ideas. Garden centers can usually suggest names, but be sure to ask to see examples of her or his work, and talk to former clients, before deciding. Do-it-yourself is certainly an option for a large remodel, but be prepared for lots of hard work.

Don't Fence Me In . . .
Until You've Thought a Bit

Would you like a fence somewhere? Please read "Fences" in Chapter 4 before installing one.

Wasted Space

If you are not restricted to a balcony, where is the best sitting-out area? We immediately assume this will be at the back of the house, but stop and think. Is it more pleasant in the front or on the side? Sure, sideyards can be narrow and dark, but so are north-facing apartment balconies. These spaces can, with a little thought, be turned into lovely, cool sitting areas. A small arrangement of seating and pot plants can be created in a too-public front yard by using fences, screens, or hedges to add privacy. Do not waste perfectly good space.

The Same Only Different

Are you good at interior design but feel less confident about outdoor work? Just remember that a patio, deck, porch or balcony is simply an outside room, meant to be used in essentially the same way as an indoor room.

So. Take a few weeks to consider these questions, since they will be the basis of some major decisions. Careful thought now will save money and disappointment later on.

A FEW BASIC ARTISTIC CONSIDERATIONS

Well, we do not know about you, but we are feeling much better about this whole design process. Having looked at ourselves and at some practical considerations, we now feel strong enough to tackle Artistic Stuff.

Although there is a lot of advice in garden design books, remember that they offer only guidelines, not hard and fast rules. Please yourself.

Symmetry

Formal designs are usually symmetrical (fixed, regular, geometric) and ruled by a sense of order and control. For instance, a formal patio might have a definite centerpoint, perhaps marked by a tall plant in a large, round terra cotta planter. Other, lower planters of the same shape could be arranged at regular intervals around it — four could be about right in a small space. An example of a formal treatment for an entry door might consist of a pot of tall pale pink dahlias on each side of the door flanked by a pair of smaller pots filled with shorter, slightly darker pink dahlias. Simple color designs rather than a jumbled rainbow collection of plants are a hallmark of formal designs.

Asymmetry and Balance

For informal designs, vivid color is often a keynote, though composition is still important. Symmetry is out, but balance must still be considered. For example, try to balance horizontal lines with vertical ones. If your display is nothing but ground-sitting planters filled with low plants, the whole scheme will be flat and dull. Add hanging baskets, a post or trellis covered in morning glories, and you have created much more visual interest.

Balance is also a consideration when planning long box planters or a row of individual containers. A row of same-height plants looks staid, but gains charm and informality if the line is staggered either horizontally or vertically. Aim for a pleasant, relaxed rise and fall in the line of plants that dips or trails below the edge of the box at least once.

It is always a good idea to repeat certain plants or groups of plants throughout the no-garden garden. For example, recurring shapes, sizes or colors — three terra cotta pots, each planted with red dahlias, say — will add balance and a pleasing sense of gentle movement. Also, balance can be created by contrasting round against linear, curves against angles.

A Focal Point

English estate gardens are often ornamented with carefully staged focal points, such as a long lilac-lined alley terminating in a charming statue that draws the garden visitor down the alley. You can use the same principle in your own little space — just subtract the lilacs. Find just one eye-catching feature — a statue, a really great pot, a wonderfully ornate pedestal — and choose a site for it carefully. Depending on the size of your outdoor area, placing the object in the middle of the space or off to one side can work well. An interesting feature can give focus to a space and also draw the eye away from less desirable sights — the neighbors' dying tree, perhaps.

Hide and Seek

You might not want to place all your most attractive features so that they are immediately visible. Even in a tiny space, you can hide a particularly lovely plant a little behind something else to give someone the pleasure of discovering it.

Proportion

If you have a tiny patio or balcony, use smaller containers. One or two enormous half-barrels dominate a small space and make it look as if it has been invaded by giants. Small terra cotta pots, on the other hand, look comfortably at home. We find that a round planter 12–15 in./30–40 cm in diameter and about the same height is the most versatile in smaller spaces.

In small spaces, avoid plants with overly large leaves. Castor bean (*Ricinus communis*), for instance, is a popular (but poisonous) annual, which grows to 9 ft./3 m tall and has huge leaves. Very dramatic, especially the red-leaved or variegated ones. However, just one castor bean plant will overwhelm, visually and physically, most decks, patios, porches, and balconies.

Color

If you love a mix of every lush, vibrant color available, great, but many designers think that even a large garden with lots of large flowerbeds benefits from a properly thought out color scheme. We believe that this applies even more for a small area. Choose about three colors to work with. Pinks, blues, and whites. Reds, oranges, and yellows. Reds, whites, and blues. Reds, whites, and purples. Pale, cool colors make the space look bigger and brighter, more intense colors shrink spaces. All-one-color schemes are beautiful: all shades of blue, or all pinks, all whites, all yellows. All reds would be gorgeous, but perhaps a bit overpowering. As well, a lavish use of variegated-leaved plants could overwhelm a small space.

A more formal look can be achieved with a green and white scheme. This combination is especially attractive in the evening — white flowers look like beautiful ghosts at dusk and after dark, while colored ones are almost invisible.

Restraint in All Things

So far, our advice supposes that your deck, patio or porch is finished and ready to be "containerized." If you are contemplating adding, for example, a pathway or a set of steps, we would like to caution against using too many different surfaces close together in one small space. If your patio is stone, steps made of the same stone look best. If you have a brick patio edged with wood beams, stick with brick or wood for any additions. Branching out into a radical mix of materials and colors could turn your small space into a visually agitated hodgepodge.

Harmony

Some garden designers say that your outdoor space should be a natural extension of your house or apartment and urge you to harmonize the two. It could be discordant, not to say bizarre, to juxtapose a Victorian-inspired ensemble next to an ultra-modern bungalow. Ask yourself questions about the relationship between the outdoor area and the room that leads out to it: if it is formally designed, do you want to continue the feeling or contrast it? Think, too, about adjacent color schemes. Would it be stimulating or jarring to step from a white and black living room to a deck rimmed with red, yellow and blue flowers? If you have vividly colored rooms, a cool, pale color scheme on the patio might be just what you need. Your choice, your taste.

ENTRYWAYS

If your main entryway is reached via the deck, porch or patio, try to set it off in some way. Make it obvious to visitors where exactly they are to knock and wait. Although you might prefer the welcome-to-my-forest look, consider that you probably do not want strangers wandering around searching for the door, perhaps in the process stumbling into a private area. Would you really want the meter-reader visiting you in your nude sunbathing spot? Also, a doorway in plain view is less appetizing to burglars.

There is not a doorway or gate in existence whose looks could not be improved by setting a pot of flowers on either side. Keep them in proportion to the size of the door.

GOING VERTICAL

A mass of greenery and flowers climbing into the sky can be one of the most attractive items of any garden, large or small. Climbers can screen a dreadful view, block excessive sun or wind, free up scanty floor space or mark off a certain area for special treatment. Mind you, overuse of vertical material might make a small space feel enclosed and claustrophobic.

Containerized climbers and tall plants, used as partitions and screens, have the great advantage of being moveable, unlike real fences. You can vary the layout from year to year or season to season. In spring, you might want to screen breezes with a vine-covered trellis and planting box. In summer, you might want to let in the breeze and move the box-and-trellis elsewhere.

To create a moveable hedge (good for mobile homes), buy several good-sized pots, at least 12 in./30 cm across the top and as high. Set them in a row and plant them with annuals that grow 24–36 in./60–90 cm tall. It is better to grow only annuals unless you live in the frost-free south, because winter frosts will kill perennials and shrubs whose roots are not snug in the ground (see Appendix I).

USING HOUSEPLANTS
TO FILL IN DESIGN

Both of us use substantial numbers of houseplants on our porch and patio to create an instant-garden effect: where before there was bare stone and unoccupied boards, there is now greenery and flowers. Tall floor plants are especially useful, since newly planted plants take a while to put on any height and mass. Most houseplants benefit from a summer outdoors, although not African violets. There is an art, however, to moving them out in spring — please see Chapter 10.

NOTHING IS PERMANENT

The size and shape of your space is probably pretty permanent and its flooring is so expensive to change that it might as well be. Despite this permanency, container gardeners are fortunate because they can plant a whole new garden every year, especially since they are working with annuals.

However, if you would rather visit the dentist than design, save yourself the trouble of doing it over again each year. Design your space the first time in such a way that you can follow the same basic layout again and again. Containers and furniture will go in the same places every year, but plants and colors can be varied. The creative urge need not die.

LIGHTING

It would be a pity to put all this effort into a place and spend only daylight time in it. We suggest a visit to a good lighting store — you may be pleasantly surprised to find there is lots more to choose from than you had thought. Lighting is not dirt cheap, but if you like to go away on weekends and have only evenings to spend in your outdoor room, it is well worth considering. Even if you stick around home on the weekends, good lighting makes a lot of sense and will make you feel like spending more time outside in the evening.

Low-voltage wiring can be used, making installation much easier — no deep digging or, in many places, safety inspections. And the styles go way beyond those little mushroomy things you see everywhere. You can even find lights to install in the riser of a wooden step, to make your deck or porch much safer. And there are neat little lights that clip onto railings. And ones that hang from curly brass hooks. And ones that . . . well, you get the picture.

Now, having fallen in love with all the exotics at the store, we still say that those short "downlighters" for pathways are a good idea. Attaching a light sensor to turn them on and off will prevent someone accidentally stumbling over the lights because you forgot to turn them on.

Solar-powered lights are easier to install than wired ones, but we are told that solar lights were designed for places like California and Florida, where summer and winter days are about the same length. Short northern winter days are not always long enough to charge the battery. Also, unless you anchor these lights in a glob of concrete, there is nothing at all to stop thieves from walking off with them.

Speaking of thieves, most of us have prowler lights next to entry doors — can yours be angled to illuminate the garden in some useful and attractive way? One of your authors has hers angled so it hits a comfortable chair from the back — it makes an excellent reading light.

Unfortunately, colored lights seldom have the dramatic effect you hoped for — they usually just look tacky. No matter what your skin tone, it is highly unlikely that you will look better under a wash of green or blue light. Stick to regular light bulbs unless you can scare up some soft pink ones, because pink light makes everyone look better. Many outdoor lights these days are halogen, which gives a clean, colorless light.

Strings of lights intertwined in tree branches look lovely. However, some lights heat up enough to kill any leaves touching them, which could be dangerous if the leaves are dry. Look into low-voltage lights and consider that one bright light placed in the middle of a leafy tree could look quite dramatic. How about a light positioned to wash a large plant from the side, sending its shadow onto a wall? Or two or three spots to highlight favorite plants?

Flaming torches stuck here and there are always dramatic — some have insect-repelling properties, some are scented. Do not, of course, place them next to anything that might catch fire, including the hair or clothing of a passing guest. Never, ever, use an open flame of any sort at parties where children or pets are present — it is just not worth the risk.

Chapter 2

Plant Partnerhood:

Plant Combinations

....

NO RULES

The sky's the limit on the possible combinations and permutations of container plants. Believe it — you can free yourself from the combination of dracaena spikes stuck in the middle of a pot of geraniums so beloved by garden centers.

We do not want to lay down hard and fast rules, especially concerning color combinations, which are highly subjective. Maybe you agree with the many park planners who enjoy what we find rather glaring: a combination of salmon orange and rose pink in close proximity, if not mingled right in with one another. *Chacun à son goût.*

When you begin deciding what to plant with what — the fun part of container gardening — keep in the back of your mind height and texture. Plant taller plants at the back of large square or rectangular planters, in the middle of pots and hanging baskets and at the back or sides of window boxes. Midsize and smaller plants should be staggered as well so that the taller do not obscure the smaller.

Place trailing plants at the sides and fronts of containers or all around free-standing ones. Trailing plants give an extra dimension to containers, softening their lines, obscuring bare stems and, depending on the plant, giving a breezy feel to the container grouping. Vertical accents can be created by training vines up supports at the back or sides of window boxes or in the center of pots.

Next consider leaf texture. Do you want coarse-leaved plants offsetting delicate-leaved ones? Large leaves versus small leaves? Geraniums have large, prominent leaves that need a strong foil if they are to be included in mixed plantings. Do this through either texture or color. We have successfully combined scarlet geraniums (large leaves), trailing blue lobelia (intense color) and dusty miller (unusual texture) in a large terra cotta pot (solid mass to visually anchor it all).

Foliage color is another consideration. Do the colors of your planned combinations complement or clash? Silver-leaved or white-flowered plants can pull together otherwise unhappy combinations.

A LITTLE CONFESSION

Starting a few years ago, it became impossible to discuss container-growing without mentioning *Dracaena indivisa* — not the houseplant but the ubiquitous spike so often seen in the center of just about anything that can be convinced to grow in a pot. Do you detect a slight note of prejudice here? Good for you. Neither of us much cares for these pointy things, finding them harsh, unattractive, and unnecessary. The whole trend is inexplicable to us. However, if you like them, go ahead. Dracaenas seem to be indestructible, surviving most conditions, but preferring full sun.

REMEMBER FLOWER POWER?

Flower color is probably the most important consideration for many container gardeners. Again, a subjective topic. We have seen container combinations we love and ones we would love to throw in the nearest garbage can. White tones down anything or throws stronger colors into high contrast — the choice depends on the effect you want to create. White alyssum and brilliant orange low-growing marigolds are a show-stopper. Pots of white impatiens in a shady corner make a cool, inviting picture. The cool effect is heightened if they are combined with a green-and-white trailer such as variegated wandering Jew (*Tradescantia fluminensis variegata*, when it is uptown), a common houseplant that is an effective addition to the outdoor container garden.

Houseplants are often useful in making up container

combinations. Green, variegated, purple or golden foliage plants all mix well with annuals. Do not discount the lowly philodendron — use it in a hanging basket with a trailing verbena or planted around the edges of a container of cannas for a tropical look.

One of our favorite trailers is lobelia — the blue varieties. We use it with ivy geraniums, trailing verbena, upright geraniums — we could go on and on. Its small leaves and brilliant blue tubular flowers go with almost anything.

One of your authors often designs an all-pink-purple-white-blue display on her front porch. Hanging fuchsias are one of her all-time favorite plants and usually occupy center stage on her shady front porch. She chooses the colors of her other container plants to complement that year's choice of fuchsia.

We have also made successful containers for sunny spots using yellow and orange flowers. Marigolds, yellow dahlias and nasturtiums, for example, make a fiery combination. You can do the same with any color group.

However, we also like to plant one variety and color to a pot. That way we can mix and match containers and change our color groupings to our hearts' content.

If decision-making drives you mad, visual variety can be created without great effort if you plant a pot with the contents of a mixed-color flat — all zinnias, all verbena or all snapdragons, for instance. Portulaca is particularly lively — good for a hanging basket, too.

Some people find a piece of patterned fabric they like and take it around the garden center with them, choosing flowers according to the fabric's colors. Perhaps you could beg last year's fabric sample binder from a decorating shop.

Just remember that you are constrained only by your creative urge, your budget and the offerings of the local garden center. The object of gardening is to have fun, not conform to what others think suitable.

PLANT PARTNERS

Having said all that, we realize that many people want a socially acceptable floral display but are too busy to plan one, or are not interested enough, or they do not trust their color sense. For them, we provide some sure-fire combinations, with names and everything.

Combinations for Sun

- a mix of upright and trailing red and white petunias. We have seen this in a window box against a white brick wall — wow.
- a big pot of mixed zinnias
- pink geraniums in three shades, plus one white geranium
- pink nicotine, white verbena, blue ageratum
- orange and yellow zinnias, orange thunbergia vine wrapped around their base twice and then left to trail
- yellow marigold, blue salvia, white alyssum
- marigolds in with a tomato plant
- white cleome, white nicotine, white or colored verbena in a big pot

- rosemary with yellow, orange, and red nasturtiums
- red trailing petunias with 'Blue Magic' upright petunias. Nice for the nose as well as the eye. Add dusty miller or carrots as a toner-downer.
- bright-colored geraniums with white alyssum has become a bit of a cliché, so swap white or blue verbena for the alyssum
- pink cleome, pink nicotine, pink geranium, with purple-blue alyssum at the edge of it all. For a big, assertive pot.
- lemon yellow dahlias, deeper yellow snapdragons and trailing pink verbena
- a mixture of red, pink, and white nicotine. Lovely evening scent.
- mixed-color poppies, all soft pastels
- a mixture of bright feathery celosia with parsley around the edges
- white geraniums with purple basil
- dusty miller next to anything bright that needs to be toned down
- kale, three or four all by themselves. Kale is so strange and so assertive we cannot think of anything that would mix well with it.
- beans on a trellis, morning glory growing up one side of the trellis, vegetables mixed in with marigold at the base.

Combinations for Part Shade

- red velvet snapdragons — tall ones and short ones in together

- pink coleus with lettuce
- red salvia and dusty miller. Some people consider this a mundane combination but if you like it, go for it.
- a hanging basket that is a big tangle of all colors of trailing lobelia
- red-amber coleus with black pansies
- black pansies and bright yellow pansies
- white tuberous begonias and deep blue lobelia
- snapdragons in two shades of yellow matched with upright mid-blue lobelia and a bit of not-too-hot-pink trailing verbena
- sweet peas of all shades trailing and growing up a small trellis stuck in their pot
- white impatiens behind ageratum
- pink periwinkle and violet verbena
- red verbena, violet verbena, and white snapdragons.

Combinations for Shade

- a pot full of mixed coleus, the jazziest ones you can find
- a pot full of varied coleus, using the cooler, less jazzy leaf combinations
- green and white coleus with white begonia
- pink wax begonias edged with blue or pinky-mauve lobelia
- trailing white, yellow, and orange tuberous begonias in a window box
- cool-colored coleus with white lobelia
- hot-pink Madagascar periwinkle with blue lobelia

- chervil behind brighter-colored coleus
- predominantly pink coleus with green-leaved philodendron
- three shades of pink impatiens with a variegated vine
- white periwinkle with wandering Jew vine.

Chapter 3

Potulation Explosion:

Containers

....

It is difficult to think of an unsuitable container material. Some are better than others, of course, but anything that holds earth and water is worth considering. There are even fewer restrictions on size and shape: if you like it, you can stick a plant in it.

Two pronouncements for containers — one personal, the other practical:

- The simpler they are, the better they look. Planters usually are not meant to be a garden focal point. Visitors should be saying "Wow! Great flowers!" not "Wow! Nice planters!"

- All containers must have holes in the bottom for drainage. Period. No exceptions. Any plant that is allowed to stand in constantly soggy soil will die of root rot, we promise.

SAUCERS

It is a good idea to select containers that come with their own saucers or will fit into commercially available ones, the bigger the better. Saucers ease the watering problem — please see Chapter 8.

SUITABLE MATERIALS FOR CONTAINERS

Of the material listed below, clay, wood, concrete and stone are porous and need more frequent watering. Plastic, metal and ceramic are not, so they hold water a bit longer.

Clay

Clay (unglazed pinky-browny-red terra cotta or earthenware) containers are the most desirable. Small wonder, because they look terrific. Clay pots come in many shapes and sizes, some plain and classy, some decorated and classy. They are inexpensive to manufacture, but the larger ones cost a lot because they are difficult to ship — big, heavy, brittle. They are suitable for both formal and informal spaces. We have never seen a terra cotta pot decorated to the point of vulgarity, which cannot be said for all pots.

Unglazed clay is porous, dries out quickly and so needs more frequent watering.

Large clay pots to be left outside all winter should be emptied out before frost comes. If they freeze while still full of damp earth, the expanding water could easily crack them in two. We have seen this happen to $200 pots. Ouch. Similarly, ornate clay pots should winter indoors because they are more fragile than the standard models.

Once clay pots have been used for a couple of years, they will become discolored from deposits of mineral salts that constantly leach out of the soil. If this bothers you, put the pot in another, cleaner container. Some people consider this discoloration desirable and think of it as an honorable patina of age.

Wood

Wood is an attractive, practical and fairly low-cost material for planters. Most lumber stores carry kits and plans for making your own. Do not worry if you are tool-less or all thumbs: they also sell ready-made ones. Redwood and cedar make the best planters, for the reasons given in "Wood" in Chapter 18.

A nice thing about wood containers is that they insulate plant roots against excessive heat. This makes them an excellent choice for high-heat areas such as stone patios and cement balconies, where masses of masonry absorb the sun's rays and reflect back a lot of heat. However, wood gives up moisture through its porous sides and so must be watched extra carefully for dried-out soil.

The downside of wooden containers is that if their seams are not firmly connected they will fall apart. Many are held together only by staples. These weaklings will give way in no time flat — trust us, we know this from experience. Fortunately, it is fairly easy to reinforce these flimsy seams with proper screws. Drill a pilot hole first or you will split the wood — then you will really be sunk.

We are great believers in doing two things to keep wooden planters drier to prolong their lives:

- line with plastic sheeting before putting earth in them. Poke holes in the plastic for drainage. Use old shower curtains or recycle other plastic sheeting.
- raise them off the ground with enough evenly spaced bricks to carry their weight. Chunks of 2 x 4 lumber also work. This air space prevents the bottom from rotting and allows air circulation on all sides.

We are not happy with preservative-treated wood for containers. Please see "Wood" in Chapter 18 for details.

Ceramic

Ceramic, or glazed clay, containers work only if they have drainage holes put there by the potter. If you try to drill a hole, you will likely shatter the pot into a million pieces.

Shun overdecorated ceramic pots — those bearing molded-on or painted-on colors, swirls, geometrics, flowers. They are, with few exceptions, bad news. The bright, flower-painted cachepot that looks lovely indoors all winter long filled with bulrushes will likely look garish and overdone on the patio with petunias spilling from it.

As with unglazed clay pots, empty them if they are to be left outdoors all winter.

Metal

Metal is perhaps not the best material for planters, but it is an option in a cool, shady garden. Metal can heat up in the sun and burn tender roots. And it could rust away after a couple of years. But do not let this stop you from using metal pails if they are all you have available or can afford this year. Remember to bang some holes in the bottom.

Plastic

Plastic is the lightest container material going. The world is full of plastic planters in all shapes and sizes. Some are quite attractive — we especially like the ones that mimic terra cotta. Some, though, are less successfully treated. Choose plain, neutral-colored ones, avoiding bright colors, pictures and molded geegaws on their sides.

Plastic is nonporous and so holds moisture better than wood or clay. It can heat up, but not enough to be a serious drawback. It does deteriorate and become brittle under constant sun after a few years. We have cracked a number of pot rims by lifting a pot solely by grasping the rim between thumb and a couple of fingers. We have also split one (it was on its fourth summer) right down the side by dropping a shovelful of earth into it from waist height.

No untempered glass in the garden, please, but if you grow a few plants in clear plastic pots, children can watch roots grow. It is never too soon to get someone hooked on horticulture.

Concrete and Stone

There are some wonderful, but usually costly, stone, reconstituted stone, and concrete planters around. Concrete is usually used for modern designs — cones, bowls or squares. Stone and reconstituted stone are the usual materials used to make reproductions of classical urns, pots and vases. We particularly like the ones with garlands of flowers molded on their sides and rims.

Unfortunately, these containers are heavy, even before soil is added, and are not suitable for balconies, porches or decks, although patio-owners can certainly consider them. Choose the site carefully, because moving them about, even when empty, will be nearly impossible.

Assertive plants — with strong, definite foliage and flowers, such as geraniums — look good in these planters. Delicate-looking plants can soften the effect when mingled in as fillers and trailers with stronger ones.

CONTAINER SHAPES

First, a word about sizes. The only limit to a container's size is the strength of the surface it sits on — no monster planters on a wooden deck, please. Remember that large ones are difficult to move around.

Lower limits are a different matter. If a container is smaller than the average household bucket, watering and root development could be a problem — there will not be enough room for either. Small pots dry out quickly and require constant watering.

If you do enjoy having collections of smaller pots, set them all in a common saucer or shallow trough. To water, just fill up the saucer or trough and save yourself the tedium of watering each little pot individually. If you do not mind watering small pots on an individual, one-to-a-saucer basis, nestle them around the base of a big pot or half-barrel.

Remember, a tall plant needs a deep container. Tall plants tend to have long roots, which, without the right soil depth, cannot anchor the plant properly. Result: toppling giants.

Now, shapes, beginning with a friendly warning: many people (including us) think swans with things planted in their backs, or donkeys with things planted in their plastic panniers, are the last word in tackiness. You are on your own there.

Plain Old Round, Square or Rectangular Pots

When we visit the garden center, we note that there must be as many shapes for containers as there are stars in the sky. Yet we keep returning to three basic shapes, which are easily and attractively mixed and matched: round, square and rectangular. Think of these traditional shapes as serving the same purpose in the container collection as your favorite gray flannel skirt or pants serve in your wardrobe: good foils for your flashier shirts, blouses or jackets.

However, when choosing large containers for a small space, select oblong ones, rather than square or round, because they will not protrude as far into a limited space. Use large square or round containers in a corner, where they will not get in the way.

Window Boxes

Window box supports must be firmly anchored, preferably into a house beam. And the boxes must, in turn, be firmly attached to their supports. This is important if there is any chance they might fall and harm someone. To lessen the weight, and therefore any chances of falling, fill them with a mix of half compost or well-rotted manure and half perlite or vermiculite. This reduces weight significantly. (See Chapter 7 on potting mixes.)

If you love the look of a window box but for one reason or another cannot mount it under a window (one of us had this problem, but the reason was sloth), simply set it on the ground and plant away. Rest it on some bricks to hold the bottom a little above the ground so the wood will not rot.

One year Ms. Sloth discovered that her venerable cedar window boxes were coming apart at the seams. She (well, all right, Mr. Sloth) screwed things back together, but the bottom seams of the box still would not hold water long enough to soak the soil. So, being resourceful (and too cheap to go out and buy new boxes), Ms. Sloth dumped out the soil, lined the boxes with plastic, stabbed holes in for drainage and then put the soil back in. Planted it with zinnias. Worked fine.

A tip: to carry a window box when it is full of earth,

slide two 2 x 4s under it lengthwise and carry it resting on these supports. Without this stretcher-like helper, you risk the whole shebang falling apart when lifted.

For safe use on balconies, hang your window boxes on the inside, not outside, of the railing. Better it drop on your toe than on someone's head ten storeys below. Apart from not wanting to hurt anyone, we live in a litigious society these days.

Hanging Baskets

Skyhooks must be firmly screwed into a beam because dirt is heavy, especially when it is wet. One of us once weighed a 12 in./30 cm hanging basket full of potting mix that was one-third vermiculite and rather dry — it weighed nearly 15 lb./7 kg.

Watering hanging baskets can be a problem, but it can be eased by hanging them using a cleat, rope and pulley so they can be raised and lowered without a lot of fuss.

It is cheaper and more flexible to plant your own

hanging baskets rather than buying ready-made ones. Use trailing plants, of course, planted close together. Most hanging baskets are about 12 in./30 cm across the top. This size usually accommodates one upright plant in the center and five or six trailers around the rim.

Wire baskets must be lined with sheet moss before the dirt is put in. Fake sheet moss is now available and seems to work well. A wire basket allows you to poke a hole in the bottom and put in a plant. Same around the sides. This is how people get that ball-of-flowers look. Note: fake or real, moss-lined wire baskets dry out fast, so water frequently.

You can turn regular plastic planters into hangers by drilling three holes in the pot rim and threading wire or chain (not rope, it will fray over time) through the holes. Or use chain and S-hooks from the hardware store.

If you are short on floor space, liberal use of hanging baskets will free up these areas. Another advantage is that hanging baskets will not attract snails, slugs and other nonflying pests.

A couple of hanging baskets gracing each side of an entryway is always welcoming. However, do yourself a favor and never hang a basket where someone will whack their head on it. Did one of us learn this the hard way? Well, she experiences the same whack every year, over and over, but never seems to learn from it.

Flat-on-One-Side Pots

You can buy flat-sided pots made to hang on a wall just like a picture. They look wonderful filled with trailing plants and are useful for breaking up a vast expanse of wall or fence. These pots dry out quickly, so water daily.

Half-Barrels

These useful containers, which cost about as much as a hardcover novel, can be left to weather naturally or can be painted black to good effect. One of us painted hers with black Tremclad (the stores were closed when the mood hit and it was the only black paint on hand). The Tremclad took care of both wood and the barrel's slightly rusty hoops and has lasted outdoors through three winters. The paint is just the right degree of not-too-shiny, not-too-matte. We have seen a few barrels with the hoops painted in a contrasting color to the staves — a bit busy to our taste.

Buy barrels that have been seared inside, as this seals them against rot. They are deep enough to accommodate the long roots of taller plants. And they are massive, making them a great choice for growing large, assertive plants such as a mass of cleome or a big spill of the tall nicotine. However, too many barrels will dwarf a small space and make it look cramped.

If you want containers of flowers in the front of your house but are worried someone will come along and steal the planter, half-barrels are your solution. The horticultural villain would need a forklift truck to swipe them once they are full of damp earth.

(Did your barrel ever actually have whiskey in it?

Maybe. Some places sell barrels made on purpose for gardeners. They might look new or they might have been left outdoors to age. Real whiskey barrels will always be available because the law requires that they be used only once for this purpose.)

Grow-Bags

To make a grow-bag, buy a 30–40 quart/28–38 L plastic bag of soil or well-rotted manure. Lay it flat where you want it to stay. Cut away the top panel, leaving the side walls — you will wind up with a piece of waste plastic about 15 in. x 24 in./40 cm x 60 cm. Now you have a big flat container. Using a long knife, stab down through the soil and the bottom of the bag to poke half a dozen holes in the bottom for drainage. Plant with something spready, such as impatiens, that will grow to cover all traces of the plastic. Grow-bags are useful only for short plants, because the shallow depth of soil allows only limited root development. They can also be hidden in long, narrow planters.

Strawberry Pots

Sooner or later you will come across strawberry pots, which were designed for growing strawberries — their underground runners pot up through the holes. You might see one in a photograph, densely planted with bright trailing annuals or herbs or bare naked at the garden center, with its intriguing contours in plain sight for all the world to see. Either way, you will likely covet one. Everyone does.

A strawberry pot is usually made of unglazed clay and stands between 12 and 24 in./30 and 60 cm tall, although bigger ones can occasionally be found. So far, so ordinary. What makes a strawberry pot special is its little balconies, sort of like little pot bellies. Small pots have about eight balconies, larger ones, more. These balconies are extruded planting holes ranged around the pot. The idea is to put a plant in each hole so that the pot eventually will be covered with flowers and greenery. Looks just lovely.

The only catch? It is a brute to water. Pour some in through the top hole and most of it runs out through the balconies — along with any added fertilizers. Put the strawberry pot in a saucer and, if you are lucky, the water will soak upwards enough to keep everything alive. We recommend using both methods at the same time. Leave enough space at the top to water that way, and set the pot in a saucer as wide as the pot's widest diameter and a couple of inches/5 cm deep. Fill it up every day, without fail. We wish you better luck than we have ever had.

Although we have not yet tried this potting technique, it sounds like it ought to work: place a cardboard or stiff plastic tube full length down the empty pot's center. Fill the tube with fine gravel. Add soil up to the first set of holes and then plant. Add more soil until you reach the next set of holes and plant those. Continue for as many holes as you have, then pull the tube out. Water through the gravel core for a uniform wetting. Worth a try.

Planting Column

This makes excellent use of a small space. It is a vertical column of earth held in place by wire mesh and sheet plastic. Plants are inserted into holes all over it, so that when they grow together the effect is one of a self-supported column of blossom. They can be bought ready-made and ready-planted at large garden centers or you can make your own.

To make one, go to the hardware store, buy one square yard/one square meter of what is called hardware cloth — a stiff wire mesh. Chicken wire will not work, because it stretches. Yes, we found this out the hard way, need you ask?

BOX-AND-TRELLIS PLANTERS

 We would like to introduce you to a useful, versatile garden feature: a planting box with a trellis permanently attached to it. Although we have seen this planter in many garden books, we have never seen one for sale. With a little work, you can make your own.

Find or make a good strong, straight-sided cedar or redwood planting box. Maybe you can find a window box that will serve. A versatile size is 1 ft. deep x 1 ft. wide x 3 ft. long/30 cm x 30 cm x 100 cm. Using bolts and braces, attach to it a framed (for strength and durability) piece of trellis 3 ft./1 m wide and 3–6 ft./1–2 m high.

Voilà. You now have a trellis-equipped planter that can be moved to different places every year. Use it as a screen to protect you from cool breezes in spring, then in summer move it to shade you from hot sun. In autumn, put it back to work screening breezes. It is especially useful on a balcony, where protection from wind is so important and where the management may not be pleased if you fasten trellises directly to the wall.

Put on some heavy gloves, roll the hardware cloth into a cylinder and fasten the edges by twisting the wires of the cut edges securely together. Fit a heavy plastic sleeve inside it and fasten at the top edge. Set the whole thing on end in a planter the size of a bucket — this will be its foundation, so the larger the bucket the firmer the foundation. Now fill both cylinder and bucket with good soil. Do this gradually, 6 in./15 cm at a time. Pour water through it at each stage, allowing the soil to settle.

At regular intervals, make 3 in./8 cm planting holes in both plastic and wire. Turn back any wire ends to reduce the chance of ripping your skin. Place small plants in the holes and on the top. The plants will grow together, creating a spectacular column of color to liven up the no-garden garden. The column can be reused year after year. Spreading plants such as impatiens (shade) or verbena (sun) look lovely grown this way.

Raised Containers

Many of us, for one reason or another, cannot bend over too much, stretch up too far or spend too much time on our knees. If you fit into this category (as we ourselves do more and more every year) please read Chapter 16.

WE CAN HARDLY CONTAIN
OUR EXCITEMENT

As you have seen, there is tremendous scope for containers in small spaces. You can really use anything remotely suitable, any of those bits and pieces that turn up and look like they might hold a plant or two. Bushel baskets or wooden 12-quart fruit baskets or wicker baskets will, if lined with plastic and given drainage holes, last a summer or two. Plastic dishpans (you can buy neutral-colored ones these days) will last a long time. Pulp (papier-mâché) pots that shrubs and roses come in can be used for two or three summers before their bottoms disintegrate. You can also recycle grandmother's chamber pot or uncle's spittoon. Whatever you do, remember to let the plant, not the container, dominate.

What happens when we find a great container but it looks awful? Large plastic pails that bulk foods come in, gallon metal paint pails, that sort of thing. Poking a few holes in the bottom provides suitable drainage, but what about their looks? Enter cover-ups. Find a large, cheap (because it will not likely survive more than one season outdoors) basket and stick the pail in it. Perfect. Got a nice old wooden bucket with a big split down one side? Put a plastic pail (remember those drainage holes) full of pretty petunias in it and set it all out with the split against a wall. You get the general idea. The possibilities are limited only by your imagination.

Chapter 4

Containers' Friends:

*Doodads and
Other Helpful Items*

Containerized plants on their own are nice, but you can greatly increase their possibilities, if you feel so inclined. We discuss below some items to use with the usual containers.

CASTERS

Every now and then it is necessary to move planters around — a big deal if the container is a heavy one. Some stores sell special little individual planter trolleys. Also called dollies, they are circles of wood or metal about the diameter of a dinner plate, set on casters. The piece is about 4 in./10 cm high.

Casters can be bought at any hardware store, so if you

are handy, rig something up for yourself. If you are really keen and handy, you will probably be able to figure out a way to attach casters directly to the bottoms of your biggest containers, but remember that casters left outdoors will clog up with grit.

TRELLISES AND LATTICE

The word *trellis* applies to any open framework designed to support a plant. To impress your friends, refer to it as *treillage*. When people say lattice they usually mean thin lath assembled in a diamond pattern. Whatever their particular configuration, one of the most pleasant characteristics of trellising and lattice is that they provide moving shade, which means that as the sun travels through the sky, the pattern of shade moves too.

Trellising and lattice are ideal for climbing plants (please read also Chapter 12 on vines), and they can be useful in other ways at the same time. They shade excessive sun and divert too-cool breezes — especially useful on balconies, where they reduce the force of plant-drying winds. If some sort of boundary is needed between you and your next door neighbors, a trellis with a light climber winding through it will create a serviceable and attractive screen for both sides.

A hot, sunny space can be nicely shaded by a lattice roof, whether you grow plants through it or not. An overhead lattice can also hide a view of a nasty mess of telephone or hydro wires.

Lattice and trellising is best made of plastic or from

straight-grained woods such as cedar and redwood, which do not need to be finished. The laths must be fastened together securely — epoxy and lath nails (short, flat-headed) are best, but epoxy and staples will probably be the best you can readily find. Make sure the lattice or trellis you buy is intended for outdoor use. Indoor lattice will disintegrate after a rainstorm or two. Handy types can of course try building their own trellis, but this is a lot of trouble and you will not save much money by doing so.

If your trellis is against a wall that you do not want plants attaching themselves to (sometimes certain surfaces can be damaged by plant tendrils pushing their way into cracks and underneath), use blocks of wood as spacers to hold the trellis about 3 in./8 cm out from the wall. This is a good idea anyway, since it allows proper air circulation behind the plant and makes it a less hospitable site for bugs and diseases.

You might want to explain to aspiring Edmund Hillarys at your house that a trellis is not a regular fence and is not strong enough to be climbed on.

Two notes on painting behind a trellis:

- Painting the wall behind a trellis is not a problem if the trellis was mounted with screws, which are easy to back out. If you are growing annual climbers, paint in spring before the climbers are planted or in autumn after they have died away.

- If the wall behind a big old woody perennial vine such as honeysuckle or Virginia creeper needs to be painted, fear not, the plant does not have to be cut down to the ground. When it is time to paint, back out the screws and take firm hold of the trellis with the plant still intertwined on it. Gently lay the entire mass down on the ground, moving slowly to reduce the chance of stems snapping. One or two might go, but not many. If you can rest the plant on a few lawn chairs or against a stepladder, so it does not have to bend completely to the ground, so much the better. Now paint. When the wall is dry, lift the plant and trellis gently back into place and screw the supports back in.

ARBORS AND ARCHES, PERGOLAS AND GAZEBOS

These garden structures are generally associated with large gardens. However, if your space will accommodate one and can take the weight, they will enhance any design. They all support vines and provide a greater or lesser degree of shelter and shade. Traditionally, these structures were made of wood or metal. If the budget allows, you can purchase ornate Victorian reproductions in cast aluminum; on the other end, you can find modern tent-like, floorless screened rooms.

Arbors can have trelliswork roofs and are usually supported by posts. Arches have a smaller roof area (common dimensions are 36–48 in./90–120 cm wide and 24 in./60 cm deep) and are usually supported by two pieces of trellis. Put several arches together and call it a tunnel.

Pergolas are similar to tunnels and were originally meant to shade walkways. Gazebos tend to be little summerhouses, outdoor rooms, sometimes screened.

Pergolas and arches work best if they lead somewhere — from house to deck or from one outdoor section to another. An arch can be set against a wall, a seat placed inside can create an instant romantic, vine-covered bower. Gazebos are for al fresco dining — no sun, rain or (if screened) mosquitoes. Whatever you decide on, keep it in harmony with the rest of your outdoor display — a wire and plastic gazebo next to a nineteenth-century clapboard house might be an unhappy combination.

Once in place, provide lots of big planters all around their bases, since you will want to grow vines up through the openwork.

HANGING FRAMES

A good stout frame will provide space to display quite a number of hanging baskets. Frames are simply two upright posts (4 x 4 is a good size) sunk into the earth and connected by a crossbeam at the top. By adding a second, lower crossbeam, pots can be hung at two levels. Use three or more uprights to make a larger frame. Once it is built, hurry and hang the pots so it will not look like a three-ropes-no-waiting gibbet.

FENCES

Are you stuck with a large, uninterrupted run of featureless board fence? Well, do not wring your hands in despair. Instead, turn it into a virtue by hanging a number of flat-on-one-side pots (read about these in Chapter 3). Or buy purpose-made hooks, fasten them to the fence and suspend regular hanging baskets from them. Hooks that hook over the top rail of the fence (rather than those you screw in) allow you to easily move the pots around to redesign the wall when the mood strikes.

Suppose you have a fence that is considered pretty strong — chain link, stout wood, wrought iron. Suppose, too, that you have an in-ground patch of earth where you want to plant a perennial vine that becomes woodier as it ages (such as honeysuckle or Virginia creeper). Since it will also twine itself through your fence, it might eventually pull the fence apart or even pull it clean up out of the ground. We have seen it happen with chain link and a venerable old honeysuckle vine. Only perennial vines present this threat — annual vines die back completely every year and so are no problem.

The shed dilemma (where to put the trowel? the rake? the broom? the watering can?) can be solved with clever use of fencing if you have a hidden corner in your space. Rather than build an expensive (and often unsightly) real shed, add one, two or three short runs of fence to turn the corner into a storage area.

If the fence has to be painted, do it in white or a pale neutral color. This will make your space look bigger. Some metal fence companies promise that their finishes are forever, but ask to see some that were installed a few years back, just to make sure.

If building a new fence anywhere near a boundary line, check your land survey and power lines, and have a little chat with the neighbors. While you are at it, no harm in having a look at the local by-laws for height restrictions, building standards, etc. Like everyone else, we know lots of horror stories.

PLANT STANDS

Plant stands come in many designs and materials. They range from ornate Victorian reproductions to wood lath creations to plastic molded models. Basically they all offer alternative ways to display more plants than would be possible if they were all set on the ground. They are also a boon to the gardener who cannot bend or stretch.

Shelves are arranged on different levels: staggered, tiered, or whatever other ingenious pattern the designers can dream up. Stands can be found in large department stores, garden, catalogues and garden centers.

One of us has a porch that shelters numerous houseplants, many of them displayed on a couple of wood lath plant stands. One has three shelves and fits snugly in a corner. This hip-high stand is convenient for watering and weeding and bug-picking. The other stand is low, like a coffee table with one main shelf and two lower side ones — it fits nicely in front of a long, waist-high pine planter.

We have also seen for sale in your fancier garden supply

stores a tiered green metal stand, a copy of a French *étagère à fleurs*. Its quarter-circle shelves are designed to fit into a corner. Put two together for a semi-circle to use against a flat wall. Quite pricey.

STAIRWAY TO PLANT HEAVEN

At the lumber store you can purchase ready-made (or a precut kit) outdoor staircases, little ones of two to about five steps, meant to be set in front of an entry door. When one of these is set against a wall or railing, it is transformed into an inexpensive tier on which to set a considerable number of potted plants. Buy two and set one at each end of a balcony. Looks terrific. Pots on multilevels are easier to water, too.

If the steps have no back support, it means they are meant to be attached to the wall by special hangers. If you would rather keep them portable, measure the distance from the top of the steps to the ground, cut two legs of that length from a 2 x 4 stud and nail them securely to the back.

PEDESTALS

A pedestal, which makes a good resting place for an attractive planter, can add visual interest to your display. An arrangement of short, medium, and tall pedestals looks classy. Be sure, however, that the whole works is firm, no wobble. And place them out of the way of speeding children or dogs, just to be safe.

POSTS

Posts make dandy supports for hanging baskets. They must, of course, be firmly anchored, whether into the ground (use a blob of concrete) or screwed onto some sort of base or support. One kind of metal post sold at garden centers has a graduated series of pot holders circling around it. Large pots of annuals, especially geraniums, are often displayed this way. If the plants thrive, the arrangement can be attractive. If the plants fail to spread, you have a pot display, not a plant display.

Chapter 5

Dirt, lovely dirt...

. . . **I**t is a plant's best friend. When uptown, it is called soil and its job is to provide the moisture, nutrients and oxygen that plants need for good health. No-garden gardeners, especially apartment dwellers, are not likely to have a convenient pile of soil lying around, but not to worry, because help is as close as the nearest garden center, grocery superstore or hardware store. There, the no-garden gardener can buy commercial potting mixes that, in the artificial environment of a planter, can supply what the plant needs.

Around the tip of every root are many tiny root hairs, forming a minute fringe. Their job is to absorb the necessary minerals and other nutrients from the soil, in a water solution. The plant's circulatory system transports this food-rich water throughout the plant.

Root hairs need both water and oxygen, which is why everyone makes such a fuss about drainage. Roots also need to grow, which is why soil should not be too dense.

The key to the smooth functioning of this vital process is soil, the basis of plant life.

POTTING MIXES

Topsoil is often what first comes to mind when thinking of good-quality soil, but it's not for container plants, as we explain below. So, what to buy? There are many potting mixes around.

Most commercial and home-made potting mixes contain a combination of minerals and organics. The most common minerals are perlite and vermiculite, followed by sand. The most commonly used organic components are peat moss, sphagnum moss, bagged manure, compost or topsoil, followed by redwood sawdust, wood shavings, hardwood bark, fir bark or pine bark.

Here is a brief run-down on the properties of some of these components.

MINERALS

Vermiculite is a flaky silicate, which when heated expands to twenty times its original size. It becomes spongy and able to retain a lot of water or air. Thus when it is added to a potting mix, it increases water retention while helping to aerate the mix, so roots get that much-needed oxygen. It is also lightweight, a useful quality for balcony gardeners.

Perlite, or sponge rock, is a granite-like volcanic material. After being crushed, it is heated. The perlite pops like popcorn and, like vermiculite, expands to twenty times its original volume. However, perlite does not retain water inside its popcorn ball, but rather attracts water around it. Thus it can dry out faster than vermiculite. Perlite also aerates a mix and is lightweight.

Screened sand is present in commercial mixes. You can add it to your own mix for drainage and aeration. Unscreened sand, such as you would find at a beach, is not a good choice because it often contains large pieces of wood, rocks and other debris better left out of a potting mix.

ORGANICS

If you decide to use **peat moss** or **sphagnum moss** as the organic element in your potting mix, wet the final mixture down and wait until it becomes saturated before potting plants in it. Dry peat moss flies through the air, makes you sneeze and creates a terrible mess, so if at all possible work with it outdoors or in the basement or garage — somewhere easy to hose down afterwards. And be warned: peat moss is notoriously difficult to saturate at first. Experienced gardeners soak it overnight in a bucket and then squeeze the excess water out of it before using it. Your authors do not like mixes with a heavy peat moss content because they are so difficult to wet down the first time (although peat moss is good at retaining moisture once it has got itself organized). We also find they develop a hard top crust, or dry out too fast or compact. We prefer using soil, compost, or manure instead.

Compost is such a Good Thing it gets a whole chapter to itself — turn to Chapter 6.

Did you faint when we mentioned bagged manure as a good organic addition to potting mix? If so, please revive yourself, as all bagged manure is three or four years old — its birthdate marked by its, er, departure from the sheep or cow. What you are buying is called **well-rotted manure**. It is not smelly or repulsive in any way; in fact, it looks like plain old earth. Fresh manure is not appropriate since, besides being too disgusting to work with, it will burn plant roots.

SOIL AND TOPSOIL

You do not want to plant your container plants in pure topsoil. Despite its big rep, topsoil is so dense it is apt to clog and compact in containers — one of your authors used pure topsoil in her containers one summer, back before she knew any better, and was rewarded for her ignorance by poor sad little plants that could not work their roots down into the impenetrable mass.

Although we have both, upon occasion, added soil out of our gardens to our potting mixes (the stores were closed and the mood was upon us), there are certain risks involved. Earth from the garden can contain a host of problems (bugs and diseases) that no-garden gardeners would not want to introduce into their displays. These problems even out in large gardens, but not in the confined space of a container. It is best to use sterilized commercial mixes.

As well, garden soil does not mean any old soil you might happen to stumble across. For example, taking a drive into the country to dig a pailful of soil from the side of the road is not done because it is liable to be full of harmful toxins and metals from auto exhausts, herbicide sprays, and so on. Not a healthy addition to your potting mix.

DO-IT-YOURSELF DIRT

The really keen gardeners among us who have storage and mixing space can stir up their own potting mixes. Perlite, vermiculite, soil, sand, peat moss, and manure can be bought in large and small bags.

It is easy to put together a batch of potting mix, but you need to be the sort of person who enjoys messy play. Do it on newspapers or in a large tub to save major cleaning-up afterwards. Mix the ingredients dry — with your hands is best, and the most fun too — until it all feels light and looks thoroughly combined. Remember, it does not have to look like regular dirt nor should it weigh as much. Wet a bit and squeeze it in your hand. If the mix clumps and sticks together like glue, add more perlite or vermiculite. If it falls apart and feels dry immediately after watering, add a bit more store-bought soil or other organic matter.

Remember that roots like to anchor themselves around coarse material, so a too-fine mixture is a Bad Thing. Many commercial potting mixes have the odd bit of bark or wood; leave them in, unless the pieces are large.

PROPORTIONS

The ideal potting mix contains just enough minerals in proportion to organic matter: 50-50 is about right. Commercial mixes usually hit the balance. Although there are plants that require special mixes, most plants the container gardener will grow are happy in average potting mixes. If you would like a richer mix, perhaps for a heavy feeder such as a tomato, go heavier on the organics. For a lighter-weight mix to be used on a balcony, go heavier on the perlite or vermiculite — see "Balconies" below.

STERILIZED MIXES

The bagged potting mixes available on the market are usually sterilized — they have been heated to kill weed seeds, insects and diseases. This is the best option for the no-

CAUTION

Vermiculite, perlite and peat moss are dusty when dry, and we do not care to inhale this dust (cannot be too careful these days). So when handling these minerals, we wear one of those paper filter-masks sold at the hardware store.

garden gardener who wants to delay the fights with pests and diseases. (Fate will supply some soon enough.) We do not recommend you sterilize your own — stinks up the house unbelievably.

BALCONIES

The balcony gardener will want to buy a commercial mix that is lightweight (and therefore has a higher percentage of vermiculite or perlite) because some soil-based mixes can become quite heavy when wet.

If you do choose a light artificial potting mix, keep in mind that fertilizing becomes an important, regular maintenance job (we discuss it in Chapter 9). Sometimes fertilizers are added to commercial mixes, so read the contents before buying. Overfertilizing can damage plants.

THE BOTTOM LINE

Just about anything will grow in a potting mix that is about half perlite or vermiculite and half soil, your own compost, or well-rotted manure. You can buy such a mix or stir it up yourself — whatever is easiest. Compare prices — sometimes it is cheaper to make your own mix, sometimes not.

Chapter 6

Garbage In, Gardener's Gold Out:

Composting in Small Spaces

OUR PEP TALK

The no-garden gardener can make compost? Yes. We are not crazy — it can be done. Composting is an ecologically sound practice and politically correct to boot. Think about it: not only could you grow your own tomatoes on a balcony but you could also use the remains to create the basis for next season's rich potting mix. You can also use your home-made compost to give your plants a refreshing midsummer boost by top-dressing them, as described in Chapter 9. Compost tea (see the recipe in the section on plant pests in Chapter 15) also boosts plants and protects them from fungal diseases.

Composting is a quick and easy way to reduce your contribution to garbage dumps and at the same time benefit the health of your plants. Everybody wins.

BALCONIES, TOO

First we will talk about outdoor composting for small spaces. Even balconies. Balcony composting uses the same methods as outdoor composting, except the composter should be kept in a big tub to keep the inevitable spill-over confined. Try a big old-fashioned zinc washtub or a child's plastic wading pool. Just set the tub or pool on the balcony floor, set the composter in it and carry on. Anything that slops over into the tub can simply be chucked back into the composter. (You might want to consult your building superintendent before you go ahead, as some managements are picky about what goes on balconies. Not worth being evicted over.)

We also have information on, surprise surprise, indoor composting — yes, right indoors.

NOT DIFFICULT AT ALL

Composting is neither a mysterious process nor a time-consuming one. Basically, you pile up plant and vegetable matter from the kitchen and garden and let it rot, usually in an enclosed but aerated container. The best compost comes from mixing a whole mess of substances in together — see below for a list of what and what not to add.

The challenge for no-garden gardeners is finding the space for a composter. Luckily, composting has become so popular that a variety of compost units, in many sizes, can be found without your having to track down obscure stores known only to keen recyclers.

WHAT YOU NEED

Do you have even a little space in some easily accessible spot — on or near your deck or patio, near the garage or carport? Then invest in a compost unit or build one yourself. (We are not, personally, big fans of this particular do-it-yourself project, since there are so many functional, reasonably priced units in the stores.)

A well-designed, small-space, no-garden compost box must:

- have slits or holes in the sides to admit air
- have an easily removeable lid, but one heavy enough (or one that latches) to deter squirrels and raccoons
- have a reasonably attractive, if utilitarian, appearance
- be durable
- take up about a square yard/square meter of floor space
- hold at least 1 cubic yard/cubic meter of material; smaller piles will work, but more slowly.

Many large bins come without bottoms so that they sit directly on the ground. This allows earthworms and micro-organisms to crawl in and help out in the decomposing process. However, if you can only sit one of these models on a patio or deck, lay a heavy plastic sheet down and set the compost bin on it. The plastic will protect wood from rotting and patio stones from staining. Encourage worms and micro-organisms by throwing in good topsoil once in a while. If you can cadge a bucketful of nice wormy soil from a neighbor's garden and throw that in, so much the better.

OUR FAVORITE COMPOST BOXES

One of our favorite large compost units is the SoilSaver, a patented, Canadian-designed box made with recycled plastic. This well-made, long-lasting box costs about the same as four big bags of good-quality fertilizer, but some enlightened municipalities sell them to city gardeners at a fraction of their retail cost.

The SoilSaver, a dark, matte brown box, blends in with most gardens. The SoilSaver's design meets all of our composter criteria. Set the composter in sun or shade, it does not matter which, although composters in sunny sites tend to dry out faster. Keep the unit out of windy locations though — unattached tops have a tendency to fly off in all directions.

You may want to screen the bin from view. This can be done by placing it in an obscure corner or by constructing a screen — a vine-laden trellis is hard to beat — in front of it. Wherever you place the composter, be sure it can be conveniently reached. If you have to go through a complicated route to dump kitchen and plant waste, your composting enthusiasm will soon disappear.

Inventive types can make a composter out of a garbage can. Be sure to poke holes in the sides and bottom to admit air, as the pile will not work properly without oxygen.

There is a commercially available 3 ft./1 m high plastic composter unit, which holds 45 gal./200 L that could be an option for apartment dwellers to use on their balconies. It is called Bio-Keg and is manufactured by Composting Systems of Belleville, Ontario. You can also purchase a stirring mechanism which fits inside the keg and will help make compost faster.

Another small-size composter is made by Environ-Mate of West Hill, Ontario. The Com-Post Aerator fits inside most garbage cans or garbage bags. Basically it allows you to compost in a covered container without worrying about odor. Which brings us to the major worry many people have about composting . . .

SoilSaver®

SMELLS

A well-managed compost pile does not smell. If it does, it is too wet. Add soil and dry material (dry grass clippings, dry leaves) and you will be fine.

COMPOST DO'S AND DON'TS

Throw in

- plants and plant clippings are always welcome. The smaller the pieces, the faster they will break down.

- weeds but not with seed heads intact — the seeds can germinate when the compost is spread next season.

- add only a couple of inches of grass clippings at a time. Too much and they will compact into airless mats, which break down slowly and can smell.

- tree leaves are good composter additions. Add over time if you have lots. Put extra leaves into a plastic bag and add as space becomes available.

- add potato peelings, tomato skins, carrot tops, egg shells, etc. Cut broccoli and cauliflower stumps into small pieces.

- coffee grounds (including the paper filter, but try to use the unbleached ones) are also acceptable, as well as tea bags, if the bag is biodegradable. Tear the bag.

- small amounts of ashes from a wood fire can be scattered over the pile.

Do not add

- dog and cat poop because they contain parasites harmful to humans

- coal, barbecue briquet or fake log ashes — they contain undesirable chemicals

- anything diseased or bug-infested, covered with herbicide or pesticide residues

- animal fat, skin, bones, dairy products, because they will stink and attract rodents

- anything salty because salt harms the beneficial micro-organisms
- paper, plastic, metal. Newspaper can, technically, be added, if they are shredded. But, daily additions would soon wreck the balance of materials in the mix. Better to put papers into the recycle box.

COMPOST MAINTENANCE

Add both wet (fresh peelings, green leaves, etc.) and dry (dried-out leaves, etc.) material to the compost pile. A 50-50 mix should be fine. No need to layer the materials, they will decompose faster if they are stirred together.

Traditionally, it has been the practice to begin a pile by covering the bottom with unsterilized soil or, if you have a friend who will give you some, a bit of finished compost. This layer contains needed micro-organisms.

Do not add too much of one thing at one time. Good compost results from a mix of many different materials. For instance, if you have lots and lots of fallen-off-the-tree crabapples, add them 2 in./5 cm at a time, not all at once.

The pile will work best if it is slightly moist — like a wrung-out sponge. If the pile is dry, water it with a hose or watering can, or uncover it during a rain storm, or stir in fresh wet plant and vegetable matter.

The pile will not work and might become smelly if too much wet material is added. The smell results when the desired aerobic (that is, using oxygen) decomposition stops.

A too-wet environment excludes air, producing anaerobic (without oxygen) decomposition, and thus a dreadful smell. To remedy this, cover the pile during rain and uncover it when the sun comes out. Also, stir in some soil or dry material or both. Stirring the pile to add air helps a little.

Pile too soggy? Stir in dry material or empty the container, and spread the contents out in a thin layer. Let it dry in the sun and then reassemble it all.

Stirring the pile makes the pile work faster. Doing this, especially in a box, with a spade or fork can be damned hard work. You can buy a special compost-stirring stick. It is an aluminum pipe, about 1 yd./1 m long, with a handle at one end and at the other an arrowhead-shaped, hand-sized piece of flat metal. Shove it in and haul it out a few times — it turns the pile as it comes out. It still is hard work — watch out for your back.

Now and then throw in some soil begged from a neighbor's garden, or use unsterilized bagged potting soil or topsoil, to keep odors down and add micro-organisms that assist in breaking down organic matter in the pile. A healthy pile will be full of worms, millipedes, sow bugs and other creepy-crawlies that help break things down. If you have put the whole shebang in a plastic wading pool, it should keep these critters from roaming away and inviting themselves to breakfast in your kitchen.

We personally do not believe in commercial composter boosters. They are expensive and do not appreciably speed up the process.

FINISHED COMPOST

Working compost loses volume dramatically, making room for additions. If a pile is started in spring, you may get some finished compost by late summer.

Finished compost is dark and crumbly, composed of different-sized particles at the bottom of the pile. During the summer, poke around to see if there is enough compost to be worth digging out. If the compost is ready, haul it out. Throw anything that has not fully composted back into the box. Keen gardeners sift their compost before using it. Many factors determine the amount of compost in your container: how topped-up the box was kept, if the material was chopped up, how often the pile was stirred and what the weather has been like. This is not a race, so relax, it will take as long as it takes.

WINTER COMPOSTING

Once freezing temperatures begin, the compost pile will freeze and stop working until spring. You can still keep your kitchen waste out of the curbside garbage, though.

A frozen pile does not subside the way a working one does. So, line a lidded curbside-sized garbage can with a big plastic bag, and keep it outside the back door. Dump kitchen waste into it throughout the winter, replacing the bags as they fill up. When spring comes and there is room in your compost unit, dump in the contents. A family of four produced nearly three bags last year.

A REAL CAN OF WORMS . . . WELL, WOULD YOU BELIEVE A BOX OF WORMS?

For apartment dwellers or anyone who enjoys squirmy pets, vermicomposting (that is, with worms) has become an alternative to outdoor bins. However, it works only with kitchen wastes and not a large volume of garden wastes. (The odd handful of leaves or flowers is acceptable.)

If the idea of a worm-filled box under the kitchen sink appeals to you, try it. A few Canadian firms are producing the units and providing the worms. The average size of a worm bin is 1 x 2 x 3 ft./30 x 60 x 90 cm. The worms are a special warmth-loving species — not your ordinary garden worm. Redworms and African night crawlers are the worms of choice. They can be bought at fishing and bait stores and in some enlightened garden centers. The worms reduce vegetable matter by munching it up and, well, excreting compost.

The worms need moisture, oxygen and a good bedding material in order to feel at home and do the work they were born to do. According to Mark Cullen and Lorraine Johnson (who have written the bible of composting, *The Real Dirt: The Complete Guide to Backyard, Balcony and Apartment Composting*), you can make bedding material from newspaper (not the colored pages), corrugated cardboard, peat moss, straw, leaves or a mixture of these. Be sure to soak the paper products for a short time, then shred them up. Peat moss should be soaked overnight to reduce its acidity and wrung dry before use.

Put about 4 in./10 cm of bedding material into the container, dampen the material until moist, add worms. Add vegetable matter and stir gently into bedding material. Finally, cover the matter with more bedding material to avoid odors and fruit fly infestations. The smaller the pieces, the faster usable compost will be produced. The worms will not only eat the usual fruit and vegetable scraps but will also munch their way through tea bags, pulverized egg shells (do it with a rolling pin), bread, baked goods, rice, grains, chopped nuts, and pasta. Cheese and oils in large amounts should not be thrown into the bin.

After two or three months your worm-casting (worm poop is politely referred to as castings) compost will be ready to harvest. Make fresh bedding, separate out the worms and then rebuild your vermicomposter. Wear rubber gloves if the thought of touching a worm gives you the shivers.

A few problems might develop when using this type of composter. Odor should not be a problem unless you are overfeeding, have too many or too few worms for the size of the unit or the amount of kitchen waste you produce, or have added too much water. Also, the mix will smell if it is too acidic. To remedy this, Cullen and Johnson advise adding powdered eggshells — a couple of tablespoons/30 mL a week.

Gray mold can form on the surface of the bedding material. This is a signal that the worms cannot keep up with the amount you are feeding them. Hold back or buy more worms.

Fruit flies can make a happy home in this rich mix. Trap them in a hornet and wasp trap (available in garden centers) and make sure that you consistently cover added kitchen waste completely with the bedding mix.

The worms can die from high temperatures, soggy bedding, too many worms for the space available, too much acidity, or not enough bedding in relation to castings. At the beginning, it may be a trial and error exercise. However, the compost that is created will be a great addition to your usual potting mixes and it helps keep kitchen waste out of landfill sites.

DEFINITELY A GOOD THING

As the father of one of us used to say, where there's a will, there's a way. Be it with worms, bins or cans, try to recycle wastes from your kitchen and your no-garden garden.

Chapter 7

Going to Pot:

Potting up your Plants

....

Well, you have designed the layout of your container garden, bought the plants and the potting mix. You have bought some nice containers and have a good-sized saucer for each one. It is a nice day, not too windy, not too bright. Just right to begin an enjoyable rite of spring: potting up.

Like any other rite, potting up requires you to follow prescribed steps, using prescribed materials. First, decide what size container is needed for each plant or plant grouping you wish to create. A good rule of thumb, if you are transplanting a potted plant into a larger pot, is to allow room for an additional:

- 1 in./2.5 cm of new soil around the sides of the rootball, and

- 2 in./5 cm of new soil on the bottom.

Generally, from four to six annual plants, the sort that are grown all together in a flat, can be placed in a 10 in./25 cm diameter container or hanging basket. The number of plants will vary with the mature spread of the plant to be potted up. Please see the widths given in our plant listings in Chapter 11.

Remember, the taller the plant, the more root depth must be allowed for; that is, a deeper, larger pot must be used. If the pot is too shallow, not only will plant growth be stunted but the plant could also topple easily in the slightest wind. On the other hand, if a plant is transplanted into a pot that is too large, the soil may become waterlogged because the plant roots do not spread widely enough to absorb all the water in the soil. Also, keep proportion in mind. A 60 in./150 cm plant in a 12 in./30 cm container will look top-heavy and ungainly.

Consider too the scale of the surroundings where you want to use the pot. Is it to grace the front doorway? Small (under 12 in./30 cm diameter) pots tend to disappear in these situations, so try a 15 in./40 cm diameter one. On stairs, use the biggest pot that will fit solidly on the step — 12–15 in./30–40 cm, depending on the size of your steps.

AN OLD CROCK

If you have old clay pots that are chipped, cracked, heavily stained or unusable in some way, recycle them into crocking pieces. First, wash the pot, then put it in a paper bag and smash it to pieces — don't pulverize, just smash. Use these pieces or "crocks" to cover the container's drainage hole or holes. They should not plug the hole, merely lie across it, so the soil is retained but excess water can drain out. Proper drainage is important, because if excess water cannot escape, you soon have a waterlogged, drowning plant on your hands. We always set a rounded piece of crock (from the curved side of the destroyed pot) over the drainage hole, with the outside curve facing up.

ROLL OUT THE BARREL

Here is a little hint: if you are planting up a large container, perhaps a half-barrel, fill the bottom half with chunks of old Styrofoam flats. They take up a lot of space that would otherwise have to be filled with expensive potting mix. Help decrease weight, too. Jostle them around a bit so the potting mix sinks down among the pieces, tamp it all down, then fill the top half with potting mix.

PREPARE THE POTS

Prepare the pots *before* unpotting or separating the plants, otherwise the exposed rootballs will dry out or wither in the sun. Be sure the containers are clean. None of us is without guilt here, but if you plant into last season's dirt-encrusted pots, there is the danger that insect eggs or disease organisms may be hiding in the lingering dirt.

Plastic pots simply need a brief soaking in plain water, then a rinse. Clay pots can be more of a problem. Hard encrustations of soil or fertilizer salts may need to be soaked in soapy water, then attacked with a pot-scratcher or scrub brush. Use an old toothbrush for hard-to-reach places. We have heard of some lazy but inventive container gardeners who put their clay pots through a dishwasher cycle, but we have not tried this ourselves, for fear of what all that grit would do to the thing's expensive innards.

If dirt or stains are so deeply embedded that this treatment does not work, go after them with a steel wool pad or sand lightly with the finest-grade sandpaper. If this fails, then either break the pot into crocking pieces or plan to use it hidden inside another pot or covered by other means.

We realize some gardeners like the look of age on their pots. For others, the white, green and brown streaks and blotches are lumped in with streaks on the window and stains on the floor.

If you fear the pots could still, after washing, be infected with insects or disease, soak them for 20 minutes in a solution of one part bleach to nine parts water. Rinse and dry well before using.

Some gardeners advise soaking new clay pots before using them. The reason? New clay pots will absorb water until they can absorb no further. So when a new clay pot is filled with soil, plant, and then water, the pot walls absorb the water out of the soil, away from the plant.

CROCKS AND CHARCOAL

Assemble the clean pots and cover drainage holes with crocking material, as described above.

The next step is optional. Some traditional gardeners put a teaspoon to a handful, depending on the container size, of horticultural charcoal in the bottom of the pot. They feel it keeps the soil "sweet," that is, the charcoal absorbs impurities that might cause rot or odor. We have potted up both with and without horticultural charcoal and have not noticed any difference in plant growth. Your choice.

DEALING WITH THE PLANTS

Before transplanting, give the plants a moderate watering. Not a soaking, because then the rootball will fall apart in your hands when you take it out of the pot or flat. Plants in flats are easiest to separate when the mix is as damp as a wrung-out sponge.

Usually, nursery-grown plants are pot-bound. The matted, intertwined roots hold on to every bit of soil for dear life, so usually not much soil is lost in transplanting. Cut the plants apart with a trowel or an old kitchen knife. If the mat is not too dense, you can pull the plants apart with your hands.

Sometimes annuals are sold in small, connected plastic plant cells, usually six to a group. These look like gray plastic egg cartons minus the lid. Pop each plant out of its cell by pushing up on the bottom of the cell. The plastic is flexible enough to allow this. When enough rootball has appeared, gently grasp the rootball — not the stem — and pull out the plant.

If you buy plants in the small "jiffy" pots or fiber pots, peel away the top edge so that the fiber edge is even with the soil line. It not only looks better, but removing the fiber helps the plant retain moisture. Any fiber left exposed draws water upwards, only to evaporate into the air, instead of remaining at root level.

A lazy alternative both of your authors have used is to leave flat plants unseparated in groups of four or six and simply plop them into the container as is. This can create a dense, concentrated display.

If you have bought a large individual plant (a patio tomato, perhaps) in a peat, plastic or metal container, it is easier to cut the pot away from the rootball, rather than trying to turn it upside down and knock it out as you would smaller potted plants. Depending on the material, use heavy scissors or tin snips. Cut down, from rim to bottom, on three sides, then pull these strips away from the rootball. (Alternatively, leave your large plant in the container it was purchased in and plop it, original pot and all, into another, more decorative pot. You might want to poke extra drainage holes in the bottom first.)

WE ARE GATHERED HERE TODAY TO JOIN THIS POT AND THIS PLANT . . .

We usually start by filling the container about one-quarter, one-third or one-half full of potting mix, depending on the size of the rootballs and the container. Firm the mix down a little, then loosely smooth some soil up the walls of the pot. If you are putting just one plant in the pot, place it in the middle of this soil arrangement. If more than one, evenly space the rootballs around the container.

Give each rootball a gentle push into the bottom soil so it is firmly seated. Then, if the container is small enough to wrestle with, bang or thump the pot gently. This causes the soil you smoothed up the sides to fall neatly down around the roots, ensuring good contact between soil and rootball. If the pot is too big to thump, push the banked-up soil down around the rootball.

Next, fill the pot, dribbling in the potting mix in layers. After each layer, gently pack the soil down with your fingers. If the pot is small enough, thump it occasionally to ensure contact. Some people water between levels to settle each one, but this takes more time. Do not pack the soil down as tightly as you can — remember, roots need oxygen to thrive and loose enough soil to grow into. Continue filling until the right level has been reached — 2 in./5 cm short of the rim.

Maintaining this level is important, because if the pot is filled to the brim with soil, the soil will wash all over the place when you water, and water will be everywhere except soaking down to the plants' roots.

Also, it is important to retain the soil level each stem had when it was in the flat and not heap soil up around the stem, as this might cause it to rot. (An exception to this is tomatoes

— please see Chapter 14.)

Then give the container a thorough watering, until water seeps out the bottom. Watering now also helps to show if air pockets have formed — the soil surface will cave in above those points. Roots that grow into an air pocket will shrivel up and die from lack of water. Add soil if needed, after the water has run out and the mix has settled.

Stick a saucer under it all and put it somewhere to be admired. Congratulations, you are now a container gardener.

ALL DONE? NOT QUITE

Just when you think you are done and can put your feet up, there is one more task — washing out the pots the plants came in. If you already have enough of this size, recycle them to the nearest nursery school, primary school or community center children's program. If not, store them for future use. We always like to keep a good selection of sizes on hand for various purposes, especially for giving a friend a piece of a particularly nice plant.

Chapter 8

Container Hydraulics:

Watering

Golden Rules of Watering Containers:

1. Check plants at least every two days, if not every day, to see if they need watering.
2. Good drainage is essential.

Water, whether from the heavens or from the tap, is the lifeblood of a plant. A curious scientist once tested some plants and discovered them to be 90 percent water. Plants efficiently absorb this huge amount of water a molecule at a time through their root hairs. Dissolved in the water are minerals and other nutrients the plant wants for breakfast, lunch and dinner.

Water pressure also performs the useful task of making the plant stand up straight — a good thing, or gardening would not be a very interesting pursuit. Water fills every cell and keeps the plant rigid. This rigidity is called turgor.

Water is busy stuff, constantly coming and going within a plant. It continually evaporates out of leaf pores, but fortunately, as fast as water molecules evaporate, that action pulls up on the molecules below, causing a chain reaction that continues right down to the root hairs.

Obviously, water is essential, but too much of a good thing can also kill. It is important to get your head around this, because if you give a plant too little water it will wilt, as anyone who has had even one houseplant knows. Give a plant too much water, however, and it will also wilt — this time because its roots have drowned. You do not need us to tell you that a dead root is not going to absorb much water. This annoying ailment is called root rot and is dealt with in more detail later in this chapter.

WHEN TO WATER

When-to-water is, not surprisingly, the question on many gardeners' lips. Many factors influence the rate of watering:

- light conditions. Pots in shade lose less water; pots in sunny places lose water rapidly.

- temperature. Pots need to be watered more often in hot than in mild or cold weather.

- humidity. In humid weather, water does not evaporate as rapidly.

- soil mix. Loose, artificial mixes dry out faster than soil-based potting mixes.
- wind. Windy weather quickly dries out pot soil.
- growth cycle. If in full growth (putting out leaves, flowers), the plant will use water faster.
- seasonal cycle. As summer proceeds, more and more roots fill the pot and will need more water to satisfy them.
- type of plant. Vegetable and flowering plants have greater need for water than foliage plants, cacti and succulents.
- pot size. Smaller pots dry out faster than larger ones.
- pot type. Porous materials, such as clay or untreated wood, dry out faster than nonporous plastic or ceramic pots.
- pot position. Hanging pots dry out faster, from the evaporation caused by circulating air, than pots sitting closer to the ground.

Yes, you may say, but how can I tell when to water, short of crunching all the above information through a computer? Easy.

You can look at the soil — dry soil is a lighter color than wet. And you can feel. Many enthusiastic container gardeners have permanent dirt under a fingernail from constantly poking into their pots, testing for wetness. Stick a finger into the soil, up to the first knuckle. If the mix feels dry, water. If not, do not.

Dry potting mix is also lighter in weight than wet. Lift the pot a little — just one side, if it is a big pot. Does it feel lighter than it should? Then water. Within a few days, you will get to know how much each of your pots should weigh when nicely moist.

Sometimes daily life intrudes on our watering schedules until the potting mix in some of our pots becomes so dry that it pulls away from the edges of the pot. Be careful when watering these thirsty plants. Instead of soaking through the soil the water will, irritatingly, run down the space between pot and soil. In this case, leave the excess water in the saucer until it is absorbed upwards by the plant, then water once again and stop when the water runs into the saucer.

OLD-TIME KNOW-HOW

Old-time gardeners, who know a lot about labor-saving techniques, keep a long stick or broom handle handy in the garden. To check if terra cotta pots are dry, they rap the pot with the stick — no need to bend over. If it raps hollow, time to water. A heavy thonk means the pot is nicely moist.

HOW TO WATER WELL

The best way to water is to fill up the saucer, so water can soak upwards into the root mass and at the same time to fill the top 2 in./5 cm of the container, which has been left free of soil for just this purpose.

KILLING WITH KINDNESS: ROOT ROT

People in the houseplant biz tell us that more houseplants die of overwatering than any other cause. This is sometimes the case with outdoor container plants. Why? Because a wilted plant is usually a sign that watering is needed and people automatically water when they see wilt.

However. Wilt can sometimes be a sign that the soil is waterlogged and has been for some time past. This is a Bad Thing, because water-saturated soil keeps oxygen away from the roots, causing the plant to gasp frantically for air. The poor plants are incapable of accelerating their water intake to dry out the soil — they can take only what they need, no more. The rest just sits there. If a plant is waterlogged for too long, the roots rot.

How to tell? If a pot hasn't been watered or rained on for several days but is still wet, jostle the plant a bit — if it comes right out, you have a *bad* case of root rot on your hands. Or you can knock the plant out of its pot and look at the roots. If they are a soft, brown rotting mass (they will also smell, to add to the joy), throw the plant out. It cannot be saved.

If the problem has only just begun and the rot has not spread far, you can try to save the plant. Gently shake the soil off the roots and cut off any brown or sickly yellow roots. Repot in fresh soil, then water it. To reduce further stress on the plant, sit it in a shady spot and do not fertilize. Wait until new growth begins before moving it back to its former position.

You have probably noticed that water often fills the saucer after a thorough watering. If this water is not absorbed within an hour, tip it out. If the pot is too heavy to move, mop up the excess water with a sponge or turkey baster. Leaving plants sitting too long in a water-filled saucer is not a clever horticultural move, as it is guaranteed to promote root rot. To avoid this, some gardeners place their pots on beds of small pebbles (in a saucer) so that the pot will not stand directly in water.

Be sure that all your pots have drainage holes and that they are properly crocked (see Chapter 7), since waterlogging can be caused by blocked drainage holes. Clear them out when necessary.

Also, if you have placed a pot within another pot without drainage holes, such as a decorative ceramic planter, frequently check the amount of water held in the bottom of the planter. If the level is not too high, stop watering until the water is absorbed. If there is a lot of water, sponge or tip the excess out. However, we will tell you from experience that it is better not to use undrained pots at all — it is too easy to forget to check them until the unmistakable stench of rotting roots reminds you.

Plants can, of course, become waterlogged simply by being watered too often — easily remedied. All you do is ease off on the watering.

They can also become waterlogged if you use a heavy, compacted soil mix (one of us, who knew better but was not thinking, has done this more recently than she cares to admit). Read Chapter 5 on soil mixes.

WILT THOU?

It is not wise to allow your plants to wilt over and over again from lack of water. Flowers usually wilt before leaves and leaves before stems. When stems wilt, the plant is really in trouble. Many plants will revive after a slight wilt, but allowing it to happen repeatedly can stress a plant to the point of death. As well, a plant that has wilted once too often will become susceptible to a number of problems such as insect attack. Each time it wilts, the plant will revive less and less. Leaves will turn yellow and limp, buds will drop and the plant will sicken.

A BALANCING ACT

In between root rot and wilting lies the ideal middle ground that most plants prefer: a moist, but not soggy potting mix. It should neither squelch nor billow dust when you stick your finger into it. Water until the water seeps — not floods — out the bottom of the pot. Keep the soil as moist as a wrung-out sponge and you will not go far wrong.

Be sure to water deeply, that is, enough so that the entire soil mass is moistened right through to its center. A little slosh of water that dampens only the surface will cause roots to grow towards the surface instead of spreading throughout the potting mix. Surface-growing roots do not steadily anchor the plant, nor do they properly absorb minerals and nutrients from the mix. Such a plant will also be prone to bugs and disease, stunted in growth and the first to wilt in dry weather. All in all, a load of trouble.

POT-BOUND

If you are endlessly watering and the plant is still wilted (but you've eliminated root rot as the cause), knock the plant out of its pot and see what its roots are up to. If you find very little soil but a huge mass of roots — usually going around and around the outside of the rootball like some sort of demented spaghetti — you have a pot-bound plant. Pot-bound plants dry out faster than ones with a more civilized root system because, as you can see, there is almost no soil in the pot. All those thirsty roots have nowhere to get water from. The worst cases are when roots grow up out of the soil mix or out the drainage hole. Some aggressive roots can even crack pots.

The remedy is to move the plant to a larger pot or, if it is already in as big a pot as you can manage, root prune. Cut away the outside swirl of roots and put the plant back in its original pot with fresh new potting mix, following the directions in Chapter 7. Or, if it is not at a serious stage, with a sharp knife, make three to four shallow, equally spaced slashes from the top to the bottom of the rootball, then repot with new potting mix. This shock treatment will stimulate roots to grow out into the new mix. A more drastic root pruning can be done by cutting away about 1 in./2.5 cm on all sides and the bottom of the root ball. Keep the root-pruned and repotted plant in the shade while it recovers from this surgery. When new leaf growth appears, put the plant back where it was.

WATER IS WATER IS WATER, YES? WELL, NO.

The type of water used is also a factor in cultivating healthy plants. Never use too hot or too cold water, as either can damage the plant. Plants readily absorb tepid (room temperature) water.

In many cities the chlorine content of tap water is high. Chlorine kills the bacteria and fungi that could make tap water unsafe to drink. This is very nice for humans, but the chlorine can cause leaves to yellow and mineral salts to build up on the surface of the soil and on the pot. To counter this, fill your watering cans and let them sit overnight. This allows most of the chlorine to evaporate out of the water.

Tap water may also contain fluoride, which can affect a number of tropical plants we grow as annuals or houseplants. Fluoride accumulates in leaf edges, so fluoride damage is identified by brown-edged leaves. If this is a persistent problem, switch to distilled water.

Hard water, or artificially softened water, used over a long time, can cause mineral salts to crust on the surface of the soil, to accumulate at root level and to cause leaves to brown. Leach the soil thoroughly. Do this by flooding the container several times and allowing the water to drain away, carrying the excess salts with it. A badly crusted surface can be lifted away, thrown out and replaced with a dollop of good new potting mix.

Some gardeners collect rain water. However, we say only two words in response to this: acid rain. Also, while some people put their barrel under a rainspout, some do not, for fear that the water will contain residue from whatever the roof is covered with. If you intend to use rain water, let it stand overnight so the worst of the impurities will dissipate or settle to the bottom. Some gardeners save their dishwater or even laundry water to water their gardens. This works for large gardens, but not for container plants. There is much more soil in a regular garden to absorb and deal with impurities. Container plants cannot cope with the rapid build-up of chemicals such as sodium and phosphates and will eventually die from overexposure to them.

HOSE WATERING:
NOT NECESSARILY A GREAT IDEA

Wandering around dreamily watering with a hose is one of the more pleasant summer pastimes we can think of. Unfortunately, hose watering is not always recommended for containers — a forceful stream of water could wash the top layer of soil right out of the pot. On the other hand, too slow a stream and you collect cobwebs waiting for the pots to fill up. Some pretty fancy hose attachments are now available that give a choice of spray and flow pressures. Be sure to get one that allows you to turn the water completely on and off from the end you are holding in your damp little hand — you do not want to troop back and forth to the house tap all the time.

As well, consider storage. Hoses are long, bulky and, even when coiled up, messy-looking. Finding room to store them on tiny decks, patios or porches can be a problem, which is why we often opt for the watering can . . .

A CONTAINER'S BEST FRIEND: THE WATERING CAN

Most gardeners do not have the same emotional attachment to their watering cans as they do to their trowels. However, a wrong choice of watering can may make the essential chore of watering a living hell. There are cans with drippy spouts, cans with leaks, cans with the wrong "feel," cans whose rose (that round perforated thingy) always falls off, cans whose handles block access to their top hole . . . we could whine on forever. You will be living long and intimately with your choice of watering can, so choose well:

- The best watering can feels good in your hand, that is, well balanced.
- Small watering cans are useful only if you have fewer than five plants. Running back and forth to the tap will drive you crazy.

- Consider how heavy a full watering can is. A 2 gal./7.5 L one is heavy enough for anyone, short of Arnold What's-'is-name.

- The ideal can has handles on top and on the back so that it can be gripped with two hands when full and heavy.

- If you are going to fill the can at a sink, be sure to take a close look at said sink. Trying to wrestle a too-tall can under a too-low tap and then get it out again without dumping out half the water can be a most frustrating experience — believe us, we have tried.

- Choose a watering can with a long enough spout to reach the back row of your plant display.

- If you choose a plastic can, buy one that is impact-proof. Many of the hard plastic watering cans crack or even shatter when dropped. If you choose a metal one, which may be heavier than plastic, check to see if it has been coated to resist rusting and leaking at the joints.

One of your authors has used three 1.5 gal./6 L plastic neon green watering cans for her container plant collection for the past five years. These cans need two hands to manipulate them until the water level goes down. Watering all her various-sized containers (about eighty) takes between two and three fill-ups. She has hose connections at the front and back of her house, which cuts down the time spent running back and forth.

A tip: after you are done watering, fill the cans to be ready for next time — this will give you a head start and will allow chlorine to evaporate.

METER MADE FOR WATER

A watering aid that the gadget-minded might enjoy is a moisture meter. It is normally used by plant care specialists, but home garden models are available. Basically, it is a meter attached to a long wand that you stick into pot soil to the depth noted in the instructions. As soon as the moisture level registers, you can remove it and move on to the next pot. They are most useful for large container plants, so large that sticking your finger in the top layer of soil just will not tell you how moist it really is. Be warned: some are more accurate than others.

JUST HANGING AROUND

Hanging baskets dry out faster than anything else. They will always dribble (usually down your arm) when you water them. Those little saucers clipped onto their bottoms never do any good, so pay attention to what is underneath and nearby — constant drips can rot and discolor wood and other surfaces.

Watering hanging baskets is made easier by using a soft plastic watering bottle equipped with a long U-shaped spout. You squeeze the bottle to direct water where it is needed in the basket. Just think — no more water running down your arm as you heft a heavy watering can above your head. Remember that hanging baskets do not have to be head-high — hang them a little lower, so they are more accessible. Alternatively, rig up a cleat and pulley so the basket can be raised and lowered easily.

Well, now you realize the importance of watering, but is there ever any relief — can you ever leave your plants alone? Yes, Virginia, there are watering methods that not only help lessen the time spent watering but also let you escape your city or cottage container garden without worrying that the plants will die. However, most are good only for the short term, not for the long haul.

Our rule of thumb is: for any time over four days, hire a responsible teenager to water the containers. If your street is short on teenagers, perhaps an obliging adult neighbor can be pressed into service. An adult might be reluctant to accept money, but a handsome present would not, we are sure, be refused.

We have found by trial and many errors that successful watering by hired minders happens only if we write out our instructions. Keep them simple. Repeat them to the plant sitter as you show how you want it done and where all the plants are — even if you think this is self-evident. It would be courteous of you to group the plants in one area, to make life easier for the sitter and to ensure that the one plant on the back porch is not forgotten. We find that a three-day watering schedule works best — with the understanding that the plant sitter can skip visits if the weather turns rainy and cold.

TRICKS OF THE TRADE

If you are a weekend container gardener who can water only once a week, consider potting your plants in a heavier soil mix, which will retain water longer. Or adjust an artificial mix by adding more peat moss (remember to soak it before adding) or vermiculite — both water-retaining materials. If you are gone for less than four days, you could thoroughly water your plants and leave them with full saucers. If you have a collection of small clay pots, group them together into a large container (plastic dishpan, for example) and pack wet peat moss around them. This will reduce water evaporation from the pots.

If you will be away on and off for a lot of the summer, grow plants that enjoy drier conditions, such as cacti and succulents and annuals such as geraniums, marigolds, nasturtiums and zinnias. Houseplants that can stand short periods of dryness usually have thick or leathery leaves, such as philodendron, dracaena and cissus. For a longer list of dry-soil plants, see our xeriscapers' list of annuals in Chapter 11.

WICKED GARDENING

Gardeners who enjoy fiddling wick their plants for long-term, hands-off watering. Wick-watering involves a reservoir of water (anything that holds a few quarts/liters will serve) and a thick, woven wick that leads from the water into the plant pot.

At potting up time, pull the thoroughly soaked wick up through the drainage hole and splay the end. Then plant the pot, making sure that at least 4 in./10 cm of the splayed wick is in contact with the soil. Put the other end in the reservoir, then water the plant thoroughly to prime the process. After that initial watering, the wick will take over. Water will be drawn from the reservoir, through the wick and into the soil by molecular action — just as it is through the plant itself.

Some garden centers sell self-watering pots in all sizes with water reservoirs and wicks already installed, but you can easily make your own. Use frayed, soft nylon or cotton rope or recycle those run-filled nylon stockings.

HYDROPONICS

Another watering strategy is hydroponic care. We find this a fussy method, because we are not scientifically inclined gardeners and hydroponics can be more scientific than we want to be. However, it can be an alternative to lugging watering cans around or hiring the nextdoor neighbor to have a quick look in your closets after watering your plants.

Basically, hydroponics is wick-watering without soil. The potting mix is completely inorganic — some growers use pure vermiculite, perlite, sand, or fine rock particles. Sand and gravel are quite heavy, so balcony gardeners might want to choose the lighter materials. Sand and gravel last forever, but perlite and vermiculite eventually break down and have to be replaced. Your choice. All these materials provide a solid anchor for the plant, but absolutely no nutrients. Happily, they are also free of soil-borne insects and diseases.

The potting set-up is basically the same as for wick-watering. The only difference is that the water in the reservoir contains a nutrient mix — nitrogen, phosphorus and potassium plus essential trace elements. The real aficionados mix up batches of precisely measured chemicals according to special recipes, but you can buy commercial hydroponic fertilizer mixtures.

Before planting in the inorganic medium, gently wash the soil mix off the plant roots. Too much soil left on the roots will cause overfertilization because the nutrients in the soil will be added into the already nutrient-rich watering solution.

The water-and-fertilizer solution must be changed once a month, because the plant uses the fertilizer up. Drain away the old water, then flush the aggregate in the pot thoroughly with clear water (leave the plants in place) to wash out any accumulated fertilizer salts. Mix up a new batch of fertilizer solution and reinsert the wick. Some growers install a mechanical circulating system, which sends water and nutrients constantly through the collection by a timed pumping. These complex systems, usually installed in large collections with huge water reservoirs, are nearly perpetual. However, since the solution still must be changed once a month, you have only swapped watering for nutrient-control.

A GARDENER'S WORK IS NEVER DONE

So, there never is any real rest: the horticultural piper must be paid no matter how you choose to water your plants. The bottom line is to keep a nice balance between soggy and parched and to remember that your reward will be lush banks of flowers.

Chapter 9

Fast Food Know-How:

Fertilizing

....

Container plants need to be fertilized frequently because they are growing in an unnatural environment, isolated from the supports found in the traditional garden. Garden soil is constantly being enriched through worms, beneficial soil-inhabiting bugs and other critters working on dead leaves and similar plant material. If the gardener makes and adds compost, the beds are also getting that best of all possible plant foods — compost, widely known as gardeners' gold.

Container-grown plants need help, sitting there all alone. Potting mixes contain a goodly proportion of nutrient-free inorganic matter — which does not satisfy plant hunger. Even an organically-rich top-dressing of compost will not satisfy a container plant all summer, although it does help. As well, because container plants have such a small area to gather nutrients from, they soon use up the fertilizers you add.

Store-bought fertilizers are not really food, although we call them plant food. Through a natural process, called photosynthesis by the botanists, the plant uses chlorophyll in the leaf surface to convert sunlight into food. Fertilizers fuel photosynthesis, encouraging the production of food.

Most commercial plant foods contain three major fertilizing elements: nitrogen (N), phosphorus (P) and potassium (K). They are usually listed on the package label in that order: 5-10-5 or 20-20-20, for example.

Nitrogen, the first element listed, is important for overall plant growth. It is quickly absorbed by a plant and just as quickly leached out of the soil — you might have seen a lawn fertilized with lots of nitrogen turn very green, then just as quickly revert to its pre-fertilized condition. Nitrogen is usually characterized as a leaf builder — too little nitrogen slowly transforms a plant into a pale version of itself as the leaves turn yellow. Fewer leaves means less green surface (where the chlorophyll is), which in turn means less photosynthesis. Thus a nitrogen-starved plant can eventually weaken and die. On the other hand, too much nitrogen can promote lush, soft, weak leaves, which become more susceptible to insect and disease attack.

Phosphorus, the second number on the label, contributes to stem and root growth. It is absorbed more slowly, thus it stays in the soil longer than does nitrogen. Phosphorus also helps a plant mature and reach the age or stage when it can begin producing flower buds. Therefore, many flowering plants need high-phosphorus fertilizer mixes. A phosphorus-depleted plant does not produce many flowers, its growth is stunted and its leaves turn purple and then black.

Potassium, the third number, is another important flower booster. It also keeps the plant growing vigorously, healthy and able to resist insect and disease damage. Potassium-deprived plants have yellow or brown leaves. Stems weaken, root growth is stunted and flowers do not appear.

MYSTERY NUMBERS

Now, those numbers. No mystery here, they are simply percentages. 5-10-5 means the fertilizer mix is 5 percent nitrogen, 10 percent phosphorus and 5 percent potassium. Yes, we know this totals only 20 percent. The other 80 percent is filler, which is often, in bags of granular fertilizer, some sort of ground rock. Why they use ground rock and not something lighter is beyond us and is a great source of irritation when we lug around those stupendously heavy bags.

FAST FOOD HOW-TO

Regular feedings are essential to maintain healthy container plants. Most are happy with a 5-10-5, all-purpose fertilizer mix. Some gardeners swear by 5-10-10, 10-30-20 or 10-20-

15 mixes to promote and sustain the greatest flowering.

Commercial fertilizers can be purchased in a variety of forms — mainly grains, water-soluble powders and prediluted water mixes.

Granulars are very popular because they are easy to apply. Just dribble the right amount evenly over the soil and water so it soaks in. Avoid getting any grains on the leaves — they will burn.

You can also buy slow-release granules, but many garden writers do not recommend them. The granules can clump together in the soil mix, leading to one of three undesirable results: roots bypass them altogether; the plant turns yellow from overfeeding; the roots contact one of these clumps and burn on this too-strong concentration of fertilizer.

Liquid plant foods are fast-acting because the nutrients are already in a water solution — the form a plant needs to absorb nutrients from the soil. Liquid fertilizers work best in room-temperature water. We have used both organic and inorganic fertilizers and have not noticed much difference in plant performance. Fish emulsion is always a good choice and can be bought in liquid form. (If you use it in a closed area, you may notice its pungent odor.)

DIAGNOSTICS

Sometimes you will need to judge if the plant is hungry or if it is exhibiting symptoms of disease or conditional deficiencies. If your plant is wilted and has a few yellow leaves, check to see if:

- it is suffering from being in a too windy position
- the soil is waterlogged
- the leaves are dusty, so cannot breathe properly or photosynthesize
- insects have attacked the plant
- a disease has caught hold.

If the answers are no, feed the plant.

A STEADY DIET

Your authors usually fertilize their container plants every two to three weeks. We try to be especially conscientious about it when the plants are flowering. Regularity is important — after all, how happy would you be if you got three meals one day, ten the next and none the next? Same with plants — fertilizing once, then a week later, then again four weeks later will not do them much good.

We fiddle with the amount, because the manufacturers often recommend too high a dosage. Many gardeners apply half the amount given on the label. Never, but never, increase the dosage — overfertilizing counts as too much of a good thing and does a lot of harm. Be on the lookout for symptoms of overfeeding:

- lack of strength in the plant
- excess leaves
- weak stems
- fewer flowers
- white crusts (mineral deposits) on the soil or on the

outside of clay pots

- algae (green, rather slimy) on the soil or on the outside of clay pots
- brown-tipped leaves
- yellowed leaves.

What to do if you have inadvertently overfertilized? Just water your plants thoroughly, letting the excess water run away, to flush out accumulated fertilizer salts.

Do not fertilize dried-out soil. In these conditions, the root hairs will burn when they contact the chemicals. It is best to add fertilizers only to moist soils, which dilute the application enough to protect the roots from burning. Also, it is dangerous to feed a plant in a container without drainage holes. The fertilizer salts will build up in the bottom of the pot and eventually burn those sensitive roots. Yet another reason to bang holes into a container or switch containers.

Do not feed a plant that has been stressed by transplanting. As well, it is not wise to feed a newly purchased pot plant. Nurseries and garden centers have scheduled feedings of their stock, so you might be overfeeding without knowing it until it is too late. Wait about three weeks before feeding transplants and new acquisitions. Never feed a plant that is dormant, that is, when it is not in active growth. If you bring in any annuals to overwinter, it is best to wait until spring to feed them. Many plants rest during the winter and therefore do not have the same feeding requirements as they did in their active growing periods in the summer.

TOP-DRESSING

Nutrients supplied to potted plants do not always have to be chemical fertilizers. Some gardeners "top dress" their container plants, especially the houseplants that they move from indoors to outdoors, year after year, to add to their plant display. This is a form of feeding, in that new nutrient-rich soil will replace old, tired, nutrient-depleted soil. Home-made compost is ideal for this purpose, although purchased compost or well-rotted manure is fine, too.

With a soup spoon or other small implement, carefully scratch the top 1–2 in./2.5–5 cm of old potting mix out of the container. Be careful not to hit or damage any large roots. Work around them. If you find yourself removing a few small roots, do not worry, because roots growing too close to the surface are prone to sun damage and do the plant little good.

After removing the old soil, add the new. Water thoroughly. If you do not want to do a drastic top-dressing, carefully scratch over the top of the soil mass, then sprinkle new soil over the surface and gently work it in. This is the same process as described above, but you are only going a half inch/1 cm deep.

FAST-FOOD SURVEY

In short, fertilizing container-grown plants is simply a matter of:

- maintaining a regular schedule of feeding
- never overfeeding
- replenishing the soil mix now and then through top-dressing.

Chapter 10

Summer Camp for Plants:

Moving Houseplants Outdoors

•••••••••••

Houseplants add to the pizzazz of your outdoor displays. They are often useful as green backdrops to smaller flowering plants, as fillers in a bare corner or highlighted on their own. They are fun to "landscape" into the general design. You are also, at the same time, doing your houseplants a favor. They need a breath of fresh air after living indoors battling dry air and low light for nearly half the year.

Many houseplants of tropical origin benefit enormously from a summer outdoors, including most of the plants commonly used as floor plants. One of us has an oleander that is about twelve years old now. It began life as one thin whip and is now a venerable, woody giant that has outgrown its pots many times. It spends every summer outdoors on the edge of the patio in as much sun as possible, in exchange for which it produces many crayon-scented pink blossoms.

A bougainvillea, rather more delicate, is also doing well. Bought as a tiny slip six or seven years ago, it is now about 36 in./90 cm across and is, several times a year, loaded with beautiful hot-pink papery blossoms (bracts, really, but let's not nit-pick). It spends the summer hanging from the branch of a large maple tree, shaded from direct sun. These plants thrive in full sun in places like California, where they grow outdoors (they get huge and gorgeous, worth a trip there just to see them), but a potted one, with a restricted rootball, does better in semi-shade.

EASY DOES IT

Before giving your plants a summer holiday, know that you must not simply cart the winter-pale plants outdoors and plonk them down in full sun, for they will die of sunburn, we guarantee it. Personal experience? Need you ask?

Indoor light is not nearly as intense as outdoor light — even the sunniest window sill, even grow-lights, do not match the sun's rays. Houseplants must be gradually exposed to those harsher light levels. Your authors place their houseplants out in a shady corner for about a week. After that we gradually move the sun-lovers into stronger and stronger light. Plants that prefer low light indoors (philodendron, dracaena, begonia) also prefer low light outdoors and should spend the entire summer in a shady place, perhaps in the shade of a larger plant.

If sheltered houseplants are put in direct sun immediately, their leaves turn a variety of alarming colors, then turn papery and die. This obviously is a great stress to the plant. One of your authors put a favorite palm in a location sunnier than she at first thought. It was there for two days before she realized what she had done. By that time, a large number of the formerly lush green leaves looked like they had been peroxided and had to be cut off.

Stressed plants, as we keep repeating, are candidates for all sorts of problems, especially insect and disease attack. So go slow — nothing worse than a brown skeleton in place of the lush green plant you were counting on to carry a major part of the design load.

BRRRRRRR

Winter departs, spring arrives, the weather is still sort of cold, but not that bad . . . How do you decide when moving day has arrived? We wait until overnight temperatures are 55°F/13°C, or warmer. If it turns colder after moving day, we bring the plants back in or cover them. You must be vigilant in the face of recent global climate fluctuations. Bear in mind that we are dealing here with plants that have been coddled through the winter at 70°F/21°C. Asking them to sit happily through a just-barely-above-freezing night is a bit much. At the least, cold temperatures can cause plants to drop all their leaves. Also, low temperatures slow down growth processes, which means fewer flowers.

A COLD, HARD EYE

As you prepare to move your plants outdoors in spring, cast a cold eye on your indoor collection. Throw out the plants that have barely hung on through a winter of spider mite infestations, the stress of dusty, clogged leaves or the trauma of sitting too close to the hot air register. Many of these raggedy, tuckered-out plants will not revive enough to become proper assets in your outdoor garden. Be tough with yourself and just get rid of them — into the compost if possible. One of us is particularly guilty of trying to nurse ailing plants through just one more season, in the vain hope that they will, one magical day, burst into flower. It is simply not worth it. Redirect the effort into a new plant.

A LITTLE GROOMING

Inspect the rest of your collection for insects and diseases (see Chapter 15) and deal with any problems as soon as you notice them. It is also a good idea to wash the leaves. Who has the time, you may ask, to even dust the house, in the midst of today's hustle and bustle? Sometimes the only thing that is regularly dusted in your authors' houses are the computers. We do make the effort to clean plant leaves, though, when we are preparing them for summer camp.

If they are small enough, wash the plants in room-temperature water. You can fill a bucket and dunk small plants. Or use the sink or the tub, where a hand-held showerhead is a great help in spraying underneath the leaves. If the plants are too large for this, take them outside and gently spray the leaves with a hose.

Large-leaved plants may need a hands-on treatment. Take a damp soft cloth and wipe the top and underside of each leaf until all dust and dirt has been removed. Sometimes the dust is thicker than you realize and is not easily removed. Make a weak dishsoap-and-water solution and wipe with that. Then rinse each leaf with clean water. Clean leaves photosynthesize easier and breathe — that is, process the exchange of carbon dioxide and oxygen — more freely, promoting faster, stronger growth.

As you continue through your plant-health checklist, inspect to see if the houseplants are pot-bound and need repotting. Some plants signal this by drooping more often than necessary, by growing more slowly, by sending roots out the drainage holes or even by cracking the pots with their burgeoning roots. (See Chapter 7 for instructions on what to do about pot-bound plants.)

A branchy plant that has become leggy over the winter can be pruned. Take a few inches off the branch ends all round, or pinch out just the growing tip. Water well and place the plant in the shade until new growth emerges.

LIFT THAT BARGE, TOTE THAT BALE

A related problem of moving houseplants outdoors — especially large, heavy ones — is weight. Devise moving strategies so that you do not strain your back. Using a lighter potting mix helps if you plan to integrate these monsters into your summer garden. Moving dry plants, rather than freshly watered ones, lightens the load. Less brawny gardeners use casters (please see Chapter 4) to easily pull the plants outdoors and into position. Or, if you have access to a hand truck, use it to safely move the heavyweights.

A fussier method, but just as effective, is using three or four pieces of short pipe or wooden dowel, thick enough to withstand the weight of the pot. The trick is to ease the pot up onto that first piece of pipe, then roll the pot forward and place more pipe underneath. As each pipe is freed behind, move it out in front. Remember those pictures of ancient Egyptians moving blocks of stone for their pyramids? Just like that.

Both your authors have used throw rugs (upside down for easier sliding over hard flooring) to move big plants. Wrestle the pot onto it and drag the rug outdoors. If you must move the pot over carpeted floors, a piece of thick plastic sheeting slides more readily. Steps are a problem, so pick a hardy partner to help on these excursions: carry the pot between you, using the rug as a stretcher.

WIND, WIND, GO AWAY

One other problem to solve when tending houseplants outdoors is wind. Tall, top-heavy plants blow over if their pots are not heavy enough. If you have a plant that is constantly being blown over, you will have to screen it or move it.

Even after you have rigged up your pot so it does not fall over, sudden or strong winds could damage unsupported stems. Garden centers sell a variety of different-sized bamboo stakes. Some are stained green, others are left natural. If the garden budget is tight, look around for substitutes. Depending on the size of the plant, you could use anything from the knitting needles you have not touched in ten years, to the popsicle sticks your kids leave lying around, to an old brass stair rug rod, to a dead branchy twig.

Be sure the stake is firmly anchored in the pot soil and does not wiggle. Whatever type of stake you use, it should be as unobtrusive as possible. Hide it among the leaves and branches. The tie you use to connect stem and stake should also be low-key — no day-glo plastic. Use a soft material — cotton twine, plastic-coated wire, yarn.

Some houseplants, such as begonia, jade plant, string of pearls and donkey tail, are simply too brittle to withstand any amount wind of and must be placed in a sheltered nook.

WHERE WOULD WE BE
WITHOUT GERANIUMS?

Geraniums are ideal houseplants for summering outdoors. If you go overboard and acquire too many of them to put under artificial lighting when winter returns, they can be stuck, still potted, in a dim corner of the basement or some unused room — even a closet — and ignored (or give them a little drink of water once a month). They will look pale and awful all winter long, but in spring will sprout again. This is worth the effort and space it takes, because geraniums are much more expensive to buy than other bedding plants.

THE MOBILE GARDEN
GOES BACK INDOORS

One of the many autumn garden jobs is moving all those houseplants back indoors. If you are like one of your authors, this is the usual scenario: she is in her jammies and slippers watching the late news, taking one last look at the world before bedtime. The news is followed by the local weather report. The nice person on the screen says, "Frost warning for tonight." Your author leaps up shrieking, throws on boots and a heavy coat, and spends the next half hour dragging heavy pots across the yard and up two steps into the kitchen. They all spend the night there, looking like a lost forest, while she lies awake wondering if she has left an old favorite outside in some cold, obscure corner.

So do as we say, not as we do, and pay attention to the weather reports. When they say frost is likely, it is your last chance to haul your houseplants inside. In fact, if you are better at second guessing the weather than we are, haul them in a week or two before that, since most houseplants are tropicals and do not really care for cool autumn weather.

Once they are indoors, you must find room for them all. We would like to help, but you are on your own here. Think they will all fit back where they were last spring? Good luck.

Do not panic if your plants thank you for the rescue from the cold by dropping half their leaves or exhibiting some other dramatic and alarming behavior. Odds are they are simply adjusting to the decreased light levels. It is seldom fatal.

Chapter 11

Beyond Geraniums:

Choosing and Maintaining Container Plants

Now for the section you have all been waiting for. Shopping for plants is an intensely pleasurable activity, very sensual. You experience a riot of colors, smells, dirt under your fingernails and, if you are at all lucky, sunshine. What more could a person ask for? It is all so exciting that even old-timers get carried away and buy far too much or buy lots of the wrong things. For example, just one more flat of impatiens when they know perfectly well there is no more room on the shady part of the patio. Thus, as with most other gardening jobs, it does not hurt to plan ahead a little before setting out for the garden center.

HOW MANY PLANTS DOES IT
TAKE TO FILL A POT?

This is a perfectly reasonable question, the answer to which will depend on the mature width of the plant in question and on the effect you are aiming for. The stake in the flat of annuals should tell you how wide each plant will be when it is fully grown. If not, our plant listings later in the book give the widths of some commonly grown plants.

Suppose you have a round pot, 12 in./30 cm tall and wide. Suppose also that you wish to plant marigolds in it, because you have a sunny location. Marigolds 18 in./45 cm tall are appropriate for this size pot, because their height will be in proportion to the pot. They will spread about 15 in./40 cm side to side when grown, so three plants in a container this size will look rich, lush and burgeoning.

But suppose the look you want is more reserved, perhaps to serve as a slightly formal frame for a small gate leading to your patio. In this case use two 12 in./30 cm pots and plant just one 18 in./45 cm marigold in each, then place them one on each side of the gate.

If a particular pot is not prospering and wilts three times a day, you might have put too many plants in the pot. The solution is simple — find a larger pot and transplant the whole thing into it.

CHOOSING THE PLANTS

Unless your will has a lot more iron in it than ours, you will become a little carried away at the garden center no matter how good your list. That is fine — within limits. Do try to keep the impulse buying down to a minimum. If you buy too many plants, you will want to go out and buy more containers. You will then buy more containers than you need. So you will buy some more plants to fill them — too many more and so . . . You see what we mean.

Another self-discipline problem will occur when you realize that because you are a container gardener, you are pretty much confined to the annuals section — no perennials, shrubs or trees. Roses are out, too, unless you are willing to treat them as annuals and throw them away every fall (see Appendix I).

STARTING YOUR OWN SEEDS INDOORS

Starting plants from seeds indoors is a nit-picking procedure to be pursued for love, not to save money. First, read a book on seed starting and seedling maintenance (see Appendix IV) and carefully follow its directions. You will need grow-lights on timers and chains (for easy height adjustment above the growing seedlings). And special little pots. And potting mix. And patience. One of your authors has tried the slap-dash approach to seed starting; she had mediocre results.

The big advantage is that you can grow a wider selection of plants than what is offered at the garden center. The widest, most detailed seed selections are found in mail order catalogues.

ANNUALS TO CUT

Of the annuals on our main list, the best bets for cutting and bringing indoors are aster, celosia, cleome, coleus, lavatera, nasturtium, nicotine, pansy, snapdragon, statice, and zinnia. Zinnia lasts nearly two weeks in water.

An indoor vase of cleome or nicotine will usually set off sneezing in people prone to that sort of thing. Celosia and statice dry well — just hang them upside down until they are stiff.

ANNUALS TO HANG

The annuals on our main list that look best in a hanging basket are alyssum, fuchsia, portulaca, verbena, and trailing varieties of coleus, begonia, geranium, lobelia, nasturtium, petunia and zinnia. The annual and "houseplant" vines we list separately are also suitable for growing in hanging baskets.

Any plant that is a bit spready, with branches running more horizontally than vertically, is a good candidate for a hanging basket. You might need to train the branches — do this by cutting lengths of insulated (plastic-covered) wire and hooking them over the ends of branches. The wires will act like small weights to give the plant the idea that you want it to hold the branch a little lower. You will need a couple of tries to find the right weight — start with short pieces of wire, so as not to break a branch right off. Leave the hooks in place for a week or two and remove when the branch stays down by itself.

There are many, many annuals out there and all but the very tallest (the taller sunflowers, hollyhock) are suitable for container growing. The ones listed below are our favorites because they are pretty, grow without much fuss and most bloom their little hearts out from spring to fall.

The best bets for shady areas are begonia, coleus and impatiens. In sunny areas, zinnias, portulaca and geraniums seldom let you down. For sure-fire results and absolutely no decision-making, plant geraniums in a sunny area and impatiens in shade. Both plants are unlikely to give much trouble with bugs or diseases.

When we tell you that a plant grows, say, 12–24 in./30–60 cm tall, it means that different varieties in that group will grow to different heights within the range given. Read the stake in the flat when you buy it.

AGERATUM, *Ageratum*

A compact plant with fuzzy blue or mauve flowers. Sun, some shade. Height is 6–15 in./15–40 cm, spreads to about 60 to 80 percent of its height.

ALYSSUM, sweet alyssum, *Alyssum maritimum, Lobularia maritima*

This plant usually trails artistically over the edge of a container. White, pink and purple flowers. (The yellow-flowered one is a perennial and not suitable for container-growing; see Appendix I.) If you let the plants go to seed and do not change the earth in your planter from one season to the next, alyssum seedlings may sprout in spring. By early August, flower production will slow, so shear off the top 1 in./2.5 cm or so of growth to encourage new flowers. Lovely scent. Easy to transplant. Sun, or a little shade. No more than 10 in./25 cm tall, can spread to twice that.

ASTER, China aster, *Callistephus chinensis*

White, pinks, blues, reds. Flowers are similar to chrysanthemums. Good for cut flowers. We hear that poor soil promotes better color. Flowers on the tallest varieties can be 6 in./15 cm across. Full sun — fine in hot, dry locations. Taller ones need to be staked. Height is 6–30 in./15–75 cm; a bushy plant for its height.

BEGONIA, wax begonia, fibrous begonia, *Begonia semperflorens*

Heart-shaped waxy green or red leaves and many small waxy flowers in white, pink or red. No scent. Pinch out the growing tip if the plant gets leggy. Stems are brittle, so place plants where they will not be bumped. The 'Avalanche' series is particularly good for hanging baskets. Dislikes heat and wind; likes shade. Height is 12–15 in./30–40 cm, spreads to about the same. (See also tuberous begonia, in Chapter 13.)

CELOSIA, *Celosia*

Plumosa-type celosia is the feathery flower commonly seen in reds, pinks and ambers. Makes a good dried flower

— just cut it and hang it upside down until stiff. Sun. Does fine in hot areas, but give it a rich, moist soil. Height is 6–40 in./15–100 cm. Taller ones will spread to 50 percent of their height, shorter ones a bit wider. The cockscomb type (cristata) is fuzzy and convoluted, like a brain. It looks like something from another planet, one you would rather not visit.

CLEOME, spider flower, *Cleome*

Lovely large, rather exotic-looking flower clusters of pink, white or purple. Sticky, spiny stem, so plant it away from traffic areas. Has a pungent odor. Full sun or a very little shade. Will often grow to 60 in./150 cm tall, so reserve this one for a big half-barrel planter — it will look silly in anything smaller. Branches as it matures. Five or six will fill a half-barrel nicely.

COLEUS, *Coleus*

Grown for its extravagantly colorful, sometimes raggedy-edged leaves. All shades of white, green, red and pink, usually appearing in eye-catching combinations of at least two of these colors. Pinch out the flowers as the buds form — they are not much to look at — to encourage the foliage to bush out. Overwinter indoors as a houseplant if you wish, but it will become leggy if the growing tips are not pinched. Definitely a shade plant — colors are not as vivid when given too much sun. Height is 10–24 in./25–60 cm, spreads about the same as its height. A few trailing varieties available, but the ones we have seen were more spreaders than trailers.

CREEPING ZINNIA, *Sanvitalia procumbens*

Likes dry soil and sun. Blooms are yellow or orange, multipetaled. Height is 8 in./20 cm, spreads to 24 in./60 cm.

DUSTY MILLER, *Senecio cineraria, Centaurea cineraria*

Attractive silver-gray foliage plant with lacy leaves. Good foil for splashier neighbors. Likes soil on the dry side. Sun. Many varieties. Height is 10–24 in./25–60 cm, spreads about the same.

FUCHSIA, *Fuchsia*

The flowers on this plant look like flashy pink and purple earrings. If you have five green thumbs on each hand, you might be able to bring this exotic beauty through the winter as a houseplant, but a more realistic approach is to compost it in the autumn and buy a new one in spring. Upright or shrub types of fuchsia can be found, but the ones most commonly seen in garden centers are the pendulous varieties suitable for hanging baskets. They are slow growing, so the no-garden gardener might not want to start one from seed or nurse along a small plant. Bite the bullet and buy the biggest one you can afford because it will become one of the prettiest spots in your display if hung in a semi-shady place out of the heat — if it gets too hot it will die, fast, no warning. Keep it evenly moist.

Susceptible, alas, to spider mite. Will grow to 36 in./90 cm across if it is happy.

GERANIUM, *Pelargonium*

Where would the container gardener be without the faithful geranium? We always, but always, plant at least two or three tubs of these as horticultural insurance against a wretched summer (too hot, too cold, too many bugs, too much mildew, too much rain, not enough rain, too much sun, not enough sun). If everything else fails, geraniums always pull through for us. They prefer dry soil and so are custom-made for containers. Excellent range of colors: shades of red, pink, orange, white, even some bicolors. Will usually survive a couple of mild frosts. Stick the pot in a corner of a cool, dry basement and forget it all winter long — if your luck is in it will sprout again in March or April. Full sun. Deadhead often to keep flowers coming. Up to 24 in./60 cm tall, some dwarf varieties available. Spreads to about 80 percent of its height. Pendulous types are available, but have never flowered very well for either of us. Buy these ivy-leaved trailers as fully branched as possible for greater flower production.

GRASSES, ORNAMENTAL

There are many types and varieties of ornamental grasses, both annual and perennial. They do not flower, but they make beautiful, shapely additions to a plant display as quiet foils to flashier blooming plants. Most of them do well in dry conditions, too. The only problem is that they might reseed themselves with rather too much enthusiasm and where you might not want them.

IMPATIENS, impatience, busy lizzie, *Impatiens*

One of the best shade plants around. Flowers profusely all summer long. Reds, oranges, pinks, whites. Double-flowered plants are sometimes available, though they do not perform well. Impatiens is not very forgiving about coming back from a wilt, so never let it dry out — it is suitable only for container gardeners who can water every day. Having said that, we must tell you to be sure it has good drainage, because excess wetness promotes mildew in this plant. Dies under the first touch of frost. Height is 8–24 in./20–60 cm, will spread a bit more than its height. An interesting introduction is the New Guinea impatiens, which has interestingly variegated leaves and can take a bit more sun than the common impatiens.

KALE, flowering kale, flowering cabbage, *Brassica oleracea*

Cabbages with an attitude — frilly leaves colored in combinations of bright pink, purple, green, white, often bicolors. Color lasts well into the autumn, through several frosts. Be careful what you place next to them, because these are rather coarse, extraplanetary-looking things, not at all delicate. The tough leaves are not edible, but could be used to nicely ornament a serving plate for the table. About 18 in./45 cm tall, spreads a bit wider.

KOCHIA, burning bush, summer cypress, *Kochia scoparia*

A nonflowering plant that can substitute for shrubs in the container garden. Fine, pale green, thready leaves; the plant has a pleasing oval shape. Prefers dry soil and stands up to wind. Turns red in autumn. A vigorous plant that has been outlawed in some places, so check your local by-laws. Sun, some shade. Height is 24–36 in./60–90 cm, about 60 percent as wide as it is high.

LANTANA, *Lantana*

This stiff, coarse plant is an interesting accent in the container garden. Can be easily brought through the winter under lights. Stems become woodier as the years pass, so prune hard in spring to force it to put out the new, tender stems that produce the flowers. Bears bicolored clusters of flowers, with pairings of yellows, oranges, pinks, purples, reds, lavenders. Full sun. Leaves have a pungent odor. Grows to 3 ft./1 m; dwarf varieties, 12–18 in./30–45 cm.

LAVATERA, rose mallow, *Lavatera trimestris*

This attractive, well-behaved plant looks a bit like a bushy hollyhock crossed with a hibiscus. Easy to grow from seed sown directly in the pot it is to grow in. Sow seeds after the last frost, although plants started indoors will blossom sooner. Silky white or pink or deep pink flowers. Sun, some shade. Height is 24–48 in./60–120 cm, spreads about the same width, maybe a bit less.

LOBELIA, *Lobelia*

Grown for their wonderful tiny blue tubular flowers, although white and pinks are also available. Tiny green or purplish leaves. Not too much sun, not too much shade — they prefer to be somewhere in between. It could take you a couple of seasons to find the degree of light they fancy. Does not like heat. Cannot tolerate drying out. Upright varieties are 4–6 in./10–15 cm tall and spread about the same as their height. Trailers are about 4 in./10 cm tall and have branches 10–12 in./25–30 cm long.

MARIGOLD, *Tagetes*

Good old dependable marigolds, great for a shot of yellow, gold or mahogany to brighten up your day. The object of disdain in some of your snootier gardening circles because they are so reliable and trouble-free. Phooey, we say. We always have a few marigolds somewhere to add guaranteed color. Keen gardeners can harvest seeds in autumn to sow the next year — pick them from the base of a dried-out flower. Sun, definitely — too much shade and they will not flower. Height is 10–36 in./25–90 cm, spread to 50 to 75 percent of their height.

NASTURTIUM, *Tropaeolum majus*

Everyone (us included) tries these, becomes infuriated when the flowers hide beneath the leaves and gives them up. Here is what we do wrong: the soil is too rich. Wretched soil will produce lovely nasturtiums. This means little or no fertilizer. Keep them a little on the dry side, too. Same colors as marigolds. Flowers, leaves and seeds are edible — make sure they are free of chemical residues. Unfortunately, earwigs also find them tasty — this summer they ate their wicked way through an entire potful overnight! About 15–18 in./40–45 cm tall, spreads a bit wider if happy. Climbing varieties are available, too, but we have never had much luck with them.

NICOTINE, flowering nicotine, flowering tobacco,
Nicotiana alata

Reds, pinks, white, even green flowers. Most commonly available are the 'Domino' (12 in./30 cm) and 'Nicki' series (18 in./45 cm tall). Most flowering nicotine will give you some scent in the evening, but white ones always have the most scent. Occasionally you can find *N. affinis* (30 in./75 cm tall) and *N. sylvestris* (60 in./150 cm tall); both are white and known for their scent. All nicotines are rather sprawly and have sticky stems, so plant away from foot traffic. Does not mind high heat. Do not worry if it looks a bit wilted during a hot afternoon — it will straighten up at dusk. Sun or a little shade. Plant them half as far apart as their mature height — for example, 12 in./30 cm tall 'Dominoes' should be planted 6 in./15 cm apart.

PANSY, *Viola*

All colors except fire-engine red. One of the few black flowers that is really black. Some black-and-yellow bicolors are wonderfully scented. Prefers a little shade, as it is averse to heat. Do not let it dry out. Keep the flowers picked, or it will stop blossoming. Height is 8 in./20 cm, spreads almost 12 in./30 cm if it is happy.

PERIWINKLE, Madagascar periwinkle, *Catharanthus roseus*

Fine in dry soil and low light levels, this attractive annual has recently become widely available in garden centers. Shiny leaves and white, pink or mauve flowers. About 18 in./45 cm tall, spreads to 50 to 75 percent of that.

PETUNIA, *Petunia*

The most widely grown container plant for sunny locations. Not our favorite, because it withholds its flowers unless it is deadheaded religiously. Be sure to remove the seed case, not just the faded trumpet. While you are at it, pinch out the tips to encourage branching. All colors except, at this writing, real black and true blue, although the breeders are trying hard. A blue-purple variety called 'Blue Magic' has a wonderful spicy scent. Needs full sun. Will become very tattered if exposed to high winds or hard rain — on a balcony place them in a sheltered spot. Height is 12–18 in./30–40 cm, spreads a little wider than that. Pendulous types also available.

PORTULACA, *Portulaca grandiflora*

A solution-plant if your problem is hot sun and no time to water. Prefers poor soil. Attractive wild-rose-shaped single or double flowers in vivid pastels. Will reseed itself if it is happy, but the resulting plants are usually the yellow-flowered ones (they seem to be the toughest). They do not have different-colored flowers on one plant — the intertwined branches in nursery flats just make it look that way. Very spready. Under 12 in./30 cm tall, but spreads about double its height.

SALVIA, *Salvia splendens*

The bright red, spiky-flowered plant you see all over the place. Often — too often — planted with dusty miller in an attempt to tone down that intense red. Try it with purple alyssum and yellow (not orange — surely that would make your eyeballs fall out) marigolds for a shot of horticultural electricity. We have recently seen a "white" version for sale, but would not touch it with a broomstick, it is a nasty, pasty, ill-looking thing. Height is 8–30 in./20–75 cm, spreads to no more than 60 percent of its height. *S. farinacea*, the blue salvia, is often grown as an annual, although it is a perennial in mild climates. Profuse spikes of attractive dark blue-purple flowers. All salvias prefer sun or just a little shade.

SNAPDRAGON, *Antirrhinum*

Velvety flowers in all colors except black and blue. Comes in the traditional bite-your-nose shape or the new, and not as interesting, butterfly shape. Be sure to deadhead — remember that cutting for the house counts as deadheading and snaps are excellent, long-lasting vase flowers. Sun, or a little shade. Too much shade will inhibit bloom. Will survive more autumn frost than most annuals, especially if it is in a sheltered location. Height is 6–36 in./15–90 cm, spreads to 50 to 60 percent of that. Put branchy twigs in with taller ones, otherwise they will flop about.

STATICE, *Limonium*

Prefers dry conditions and so is ideal for container culture. White, yellows, pinks, mauves, purples. One of the most popular everlastings — the flowers are sold as dried bouquets. Cut it when it is fully open and hang upside down somewhere airy to dry. Will last for years. Other everlastings are strawflower, scabiosa, rose everlasting, globe amaranth. Full sun, rich soil. To 24 in./60 cm tall.

VERBENA, *Verbena*

Useful for its range of intense colors: reds, pinks, purples, mauves and white. Prefers poor soil — too rich a soil will produce all leaves and few flowers. Be sure to deadhead. A good plant for hot, sunny areas. Height is 12 in./30 cm, it will sprawl sideways to about 150 percent of that.

ZINNIA, *Zinnia*

Excellent color range. The stems and leaves are quite stiff and scratchy. Good for cutting. Often confused with dahlias, which are much softer. Very good in dry, hot areas. Height is 10–30 in./25–75 cm, spreads to nearly the same as its height.

STRANGERS WHEN WE MEET

Can you say . . . xeriscaping? As we have become more aware that we use more water than the planet can afford, xeriscaping has become increasingly popular. Xeriscaping simply means gardening with plants that do well in dry conditions. And containers tend to be rather dry, as you will have realized with all our haranguing about frequent watering. Should you come across an unfamiliar plant and wonder if it is suitable for dry-soil culture, and therefore suitable for container-growing, you can usually tell by looking at it. Dry-soil lovers tend to have one or more of these leaf characteristics:

- grayish
- hairy
- succulent (thick, fleshy)
- tough, leathery
- finely divided, feathery, ferny, narrow (they have a small surface area and thus give off less water to the air)

Although you cannot see this, dry-soil lovers also have long, deep tap roots, so they can search out deep-lying water.

THE XERISCAPER'S QUICK-LIST
OF FLOWERING ANNUALS

If you want to cut your watering chores down to once or twice a week instead of daily, try plants such as those listed below, which are especially adapted to growing in dry soil. They are all annuals, and so are appropriate for container gardens. We have put these in a separate list because they are not as readily available as the annuals on our main list. They may have to be hunted down — mainly in seed catalogues. If you are away from home a lot but would like a pretty display when you are there, growing these plants from seed might be worthwhile. We sure hope you like daisy-shaped flowers.

AFRICAN DAISY, *Arctotis stoechadifolia*

Classic daisy flower in pinks, reds, yellows, white. Ringed center, petals often striped. Full sun, but not too hot. Long-lasting cut flowers 10 in./25 cm tall.

ASTER

See our main list of annuals earlier.

BABY'S BREATH, *Gypsophila elegans*

Many small white flowers (infrequently, red or pink ones). This one is an annual; its perennial relative is used in florists' bouquets. Best used as an accent, perhaps with geraniums, since it is a shy, retiring sort of plant. Sun or a little shade. Does not mind heat. Height is 18–30 in./45–75 cm.

CALIFORNIA POPPY, *Eschscholzia californica*

Flat, deep yellow, orange or red poppy with ferny gray-green foliage. Some varieties have ruffled edges or are bicolored. Prefers cooler weather, so much so that if the weather heats up and the plants yellow, you had best throw them away, as they will not recover. A spreading plant, 12–24 in./30–60 cm tall.

CAPE MARIGOLD, *Dimorphotheca sinuata*

White, buff, or yellow daisy, gray-green foliage. If starting from seeds, keep them a few degrees below room temperature. Height is 4–12 in./10–30 cm.

CHINESE FORGET-ME-NOT, *Cynoglossom amabile*

Lots of tiny blue flowers on a plant 18–24 in./45–60 cm tall. Does not mind a little shade. Will likely reseed itself for next year.

CORNFLOWER, bachelor button, *Centaurea cyanus*

Frothy white, blue, or pink flowers. Gray-green leaves. Very nice for cutting. Light soil, prefers cool weather. Height is 24 in./60 cm.

COSMOS, *Cosmos bipinnatus*

Nice big airy plant, billows and burgeons most attractively. Daisy-like flower in white, orange, burnt orange, magenta. One of us hates orange flowers but makes an exception for cosmos, especially the vibrant, exciting burnt orange one. Often found in flats at the garden center. Height is 12–48 in./30–120 cm.

FEVERFEW, matricaria, *Matricaria capensis*

Small white daisies with a large yellow center. Some cushion-types available. Makes a good cut flower. Pungent scent. In milder climates it sprouts again the next spring. Full sun or a little shade. Height is 6–24 in./15–60 cm.

GAZANIA, treasure flower, *Gazania rigens*

Daisy-like flower, all colors except blue, often with an interesting darker ring around its center. Petals close when the sun disappears. Deadhead. Good houseplants — take cuttings in August. This is a good plant for hot, dry locations. Height is 8–10 in./20–25 cm.

GERANIUM, *Pelargonium*

See our main list of annuals earlier.

GLOBE AMARANTH, gomphrena, *Gomphrena globosa*

Fuzzy magenta flowers. White, pinks, purples. Buy started plants, since seeds are uncooperative. Good for air-drying. Good for hot locations. Height is 6–18 in./15–45 cm.

GOLDEN COREOPSIS, calliopsis, *Coreopsis tinctoria*

Yellow daisy with red center, or other combinations of red, yellow, purple, orange. Good for cutting. Deadhead to promote more flowering. Not very fond of hot locations. Height is 8–36 in./20–90 cm.

ICELAND POPPY, *Papaver nudicale*

Flat, four-petaled, silky-looking flowers in intense pastels, orange, pink, yellow, white. Fragrant, with a fuzzy center. Deadhead to keep bloom coming. Height is 12 in./30 cm.

PERIWINKLE, Madagascar periwinkle, *Catharanthus roseus*

Does not, mercifully, look anything like a daisy. See our main list of annuals earlier.

PETUNIA, *Petunia*

The 'Flash' series of hybridized petunias is more drought-tolerant than the other varieties (see our main list of annuals earlier). Usual petunia size and colors. Does not mind a little shade.

PORTULACA, *Portulaca grandiflora*

See our main list of annuals earlier.

SHIRLEY POPPY, *Papaver rhoeas*

White, pinks, reds, bicolors. Some are picotee. Singles and doubles. Good for cutting. Does not like to be transplanted, so start from seed in its permanent pot or buy it in single-cell flats. Height is 18 in./45 cm.

STATICE, *Limonium*

See our main list of annuals earlier.

STRAWFLOWER, *Helichrysum bracteatum*

Many small petals, rather like a chrysanthemum, only prickly. Reds, pinks, yellows, white. For dried flowers, cut when color is best and hang upside down. Lasts for years, but if you can figure out how to dust it, please let us know. Height is 12–36 in./30–90 cm.

SUNFLOWER, *Helianthus annuus*

Coarse plant, daisy-like flowers, usually yellow, some deep reds. Some smaller varieties (24 in./60 cm), some taller (12 ft./4 m), some in between. The 12-footers are not really suitable for container culture, but if you have a half-barrel and really love the giants, give them a try. Might need a big, strong stake. A row of them makes a very serviceable fence.

SWAN RIVER DAISY, *Brachycome iberidifolia*

White, pink, blue, lavender flowers, ferny foliage. A long-lasting cut flower. If it stops flowering during the hottest part of the summer, prune it back hard and it will blossom again when the weather cools off. Height is 8–18 in./20–45 cm.

Chapter 12

Onwards and Upwards:

Vines

....

When you think vertically, your thoughts turn to vines, natural space extenders. They add an extra dimension to the garden design and can tie different elements of your space together. They make excellent backdrops for groupings of container plants and can also be used as screens — hiding an objectionable view, your composter, any ugly house wall or simply dividing one area from another.

Vines can also be used as sunscreens. One of our relatives created a shady retreat out of a small back deck by training ornamental grape vines, vigorous climbers, up one side and across the top to meet the roof of the house. The effect was so successful that their first support system of heavy rope and a few laths was soon replaced by strong side and roof supports.

New little plants starting life at the bottom of a trellis need a hand up — as the shoots grow, weave them around the supports or fasten them loosely with twine or twist-ties. After they are a foot or two (30–60 cm) tall, they will probably be able to take care of themselves. Sweet peas seem a bit dim about this and will need to be checked now and then throughout the summer.

Trellises look better if they are not too thickly planted — that is, you should be able to see the trellis itself in spots, even in the middle of summer. This open, light look works better in a small space than a thick, looming, impenetrable mass of greenery.

MORE QUESTIONS

When planning to plant a vine, first decide if it is to be a permanent or transitory member of your landscape and how it will be used. Do you want a dense vine to screen a view of your neighbor's collection of plastic birdbaths? Do you want a white flowering vine to complement and act as a backdrop for a display of scarlet geraniums? Do you want to grow a food-bearing vine — that is, a variety that literally allows you to enjoy the fruits of your labors?

Growing vines in containers means using annuals, supports, and deep pots for optimum root growth.

LEAN ON ME

Another important consideration is support. Trellises are the main choice — we discuss them in Chapter 4. However, there are alternatives if you have a handy wall.

Attach wires (about the same gauge as a coat hanger) to walls in a regular pattern through a system of screw eyes. If the wires are sturdy enough, you can grow heavy vines on them. As well, strips of wood lath can be attached directly to a wall, fence or other sturdy support. Be sure they are held out an inch/a couple of centimeters or so from the wall — use angle brackets or small wood blocks as spacers. This space allows air circulation and discourages insect colonies from setting up residence in these sheltered places. Use screws rather than nails to attach the laths, because screws can be backed out (and then screwed back in) if you ever need to detach the supports. The laths, vine and all, can be laid carefully on the ground during the painting or repairing.

Lighter vines will climb a tomato cage or a teepee of sticks stuck into their pot.

ON-GOING CARE

Over the course of the summer, check all vines to ensure that the stems are growing in the direction you want. The object is to create a balanced look.

Cultivate annual vines as you would any annual.

Come autumn, pull them off their supports, chop them up and compost them.

BLACK-EYED SUSAN VINE, *Thunbergia alata*

Grows to 3–4 ft./1–1.2 m. Twines around its support. Tubular flowers are bright orange or white, with blackish purple throats. Mid-green, heart-shaped leaves. Prefers partial shade, average potting mix and average moisture. This lightweight vine can be bought in pots in garden centers. Susceptible to spider mites. Forms hard, rather sharp seed cases and will spit them into the air with some force when ripe. Not too fond of high heat. You can overwinter this vine indoors after it finishes flowering for the season; cut it back nearly to the soil line before potting it up.

CARDINAL CREEPER, *Ipomea cardinalis*

Its characteristic leaves are a show-stopper — thin, fringed, ferny-looking. Tubular flowers are a spectacular scarlet red, 1.5 in./4 cm across. Grows to 20 ft./6 m in sun, partial shade. Fine in average potting mix, but do not let it dry out. Start these annual vines from seed — soak them overnight before planting. Occasionally you might find it for sale in a pot. They are vigorous twiners, which need to be planted 24 in./60 cm apart.

CLIMBING NASTURTIUM, *Tropaeolum majus*

Broad, almost circular bright green leaves on a 10 ft./3 m vine. The flowers — yellow, orange, red — are five-lobed and broad with a spur on the back. The edible leaves have a spicy flavor that gives salads a different taste. Sunny location and average or poor potting mix. Do not let it dry out. This is the climbing version of the popular garden annual. They must be started from seed because, unlike the upright forms, they are not offered in flats at the nursery. They need to be led onto and around a support. You might find them to be less willing to thrive than the upright nasturtiums. Watch out for black aphids.

HYACINTH BEAN, *Dolichos lablab*

Similar to scarlet runner bean, but the flowers are a bright, pretty mauve. Decorative seed pods. Grows 10–20 feet/3–7 m in full sun. It can be grown in a little shade, but flowering will be reduced. Average soil and moisture. Can be difficult to find, but it is worth the effort because it is so beautiful: once the pretty pea-blossom-shaped flowers fade they turn into edible pods of the most wonderful red-purple you ever saw. Seedlings do not transplant well, so grow from seed.

MORNING GLORY, *Ipomoea purpurea*

Grows to at least 12 ft./4 m, twining around its support. Fresh green heart-shaped leaves. Flowers range from a deep blue, white and pink to lavender. Prefers full sun and poor soil; in fact, if you are kind enough to give it good soil it will refuse to flower, so do not fertilize it. Try to do a person a favor . . . Keep it well watered. Morning glories are strong growers and quickly cover a trellis, fence or even a handstrung string arrangement. They do not begin blooming until late summer, but then do not stop until frost. Grow from seed; they are not sold in pots because they do not enjoy being transplanted. Seeds are slow to germinate: soak them in warm water for a day until the seed coats are weakened or a rootlet appears. Plant immediately where they are to grow. Sometimes falls victim to spider mites and aphids. Use as a trailer or climber. If you want the classic big blue one, look for 'Heavenly Blue.' However, search the garden centers early, before the growing season is far advanced, because this variety is extremely popular and disappears quickly. The pinks and purples are smaller-flowered than good old 'Heavenly.' There is also 'Moonflower,' which is white. A dwarf form, *Convolvulus tricolor*, is especially good in containers.

POTATO VINE, *Solanum jasminoides*

Not as common as it ought to be, this very attractive, restrained little vine will enhance any planter. It bears white flowers that look like potato blossoms, hence its name. Full sun, average soil. Grows about 18 in./46 cm long.

SCARLET RUNNER BEAN, *Phaseolus coccineus*

Can grow over 16 ft./5 m. A leguminous vine that twines around a support. Brilliant red flowers look like typical bean flowers. Full sun, average soil, keep well watered. An inexpensive, old-fashioned favorite used to screen a porch or cover an ugly fence. Easy to grow from seed, the vines are vigorous and prolific. Eat the beans if you pick them when young and slender — mature beans are starchy and woody. Whether you eat them or not, keep the beans picked to keep the flowers coming. A good plant for kids, but do not let them handle the chemically treated seed.

SWEET PEA, *Lathyrus odoratus*

A smaller, lighter vine, which grows to 6 ft./2 m. Prefers full sun or some shade, and rich soil. Do not let it dry out. One of your authors keeps trying to grow this vine, year after year, but it just does not seem to like her however closely she follows the rules. This does not deter her, because the lovely flowers (so many colors! such a scent!) are worth any struggle. They do not like extreme heat, so do not grow them up a brick or metal wall or fence. May need to be manually attached to a support from time to time during the season. Needs deep, rich soil, so use a big pot. Mulch to keep roots cool. Some varieties can take a little more heat than others and are marked "heat resistant" on the label. The more you cut the flowers for indoor display, the more the plant will produce.

"HOUSEPLANT" VINES

Here is a brief list of what we call "houseplant" vines — those invaluable foliage accents you can tuck into a pot or window box of annuals. Buy these vines in spring when making up your containers. Be sure to match the growing conditions of all plant combinations. In autumn either pot them up as houseplants or compost them along with your other defunct plants.

ASPARAGUS FERN, *Asparagus*

Lovely deep green foliage, fine textured, trailing habit. It is not a true fern. Different species have slightly different looks, but they all need good drainage and neither too much nor too little sun. Not fond of excessive heat. 'Smilax' is an asparagus variety often used by professional florists as a trailing accent. The arching stems of 'Sprenger' asparagus grow up to 6 ft./2 m if your luck is in.

ENGLISH IVY, *Hedera helix*

An old indoor favorite. Darkish green with a touch of gray is the most common leaf color. Some variegated varieties as well as miniature-leaved varieties are sold. Sun or shade. Do not let it dry out. Watch for red spider mite.

EUONYMUS, *Euonymus fortunei 'Gracilis'*

Often available in a variegated form — dark green with cream or white markings. Full sun, part shade. Will survive a mild frost. Expensive.

GRAPE IVY, *Cissus rhombifolia*

Glossy, toothy leaves with bronze undertones. Useful because it will grow in either sun or shade. Especially good for pot culture because it does not like its soil to be too damp.

VINCA VINE, *Vinca major, V. minor*

Major has shiny oval leaves, sometimes variegated, and small blue-lavender flowers. Minor is similar, except it has smaller, oblong leaves and is usually planted as a perennial ground cover. Sun or shade. (This is a completely different plant from Madagascar periwinkle, the flowering annual sold as both *Catharanthus roseus* and *Vinca rosea*.)

WANDERING JEW, *Zebrina pendula*

At least half a dozen different plants are sold as wandering Jew, usually as houseplants. This is the one we are most familiar with: pointed oval leaves subtly striped with green, silver-white and purple. When growing outdoors, place in not too much sun, not too much shade.

Chapter 13

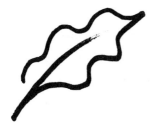

Repeat Customers:

Summer Bulbs

....

SPRING BULBS? MAYBE NOT . . .

Spring flowering bulbs such as tulips, daffodils, crocus and hyacinth are an uplifting sight for the winter-weary heart. However, spring bulbs are best grown in regular, in-ground flowerbeds. In a cold-winter climate, spring bulbs planted in containers or window boxes in autumn and left outdoors all winter on a deck, balcony, porch or patio cannot be expected to bloom the following spring.

Snow and ice inevitably accumulate on top of the containers and melt into the soil because of unseasonable winter warming or the action of the sun's rays. This subjects the bulbs to high levels of moisture that cannot drain away because the soil in the bottom of the container is likely to be frozen solid. The soil becomes soggier and soggier, as it repeatedly freezes then thaws, until finally the overwatered, inadequately drained bulbs turn into a soggy, rotten black mass. Not a pretty sight.

Yes, you could put spring bulbs in containers and put them out on, say, the patio surrounded by masses of protective insulation, such as bales of straw. Doable, and might work, but an awful lot of fuss and mess. What do you propose to do with the bales when it is all over?

And, yes again, spring bulbs can be forced indoors in pots, but producing enough to make a decent show for outdoors would be a massive undertaking. Besides, they would flower while snow was still on the ground and be more susceptible than their outdoor cousins to frost.

It is easier to buy bulbs in bloom in local stores and enjoy them in your home. Your outdoor room will just have to wait a little while longer for some floral companions.

HOW ABOUT SOME NICE SUMMER BULBS INSTEAD?

The most reliable bulbs (we deal also with tubers and other plants having food-storing roots, but for brevity will just say bulbs) for cold-climate, no-garden gardens are the summer bloomers. One of their greatest advantages is that, if treated right, they will bloom for many years in succession.

They can be bought in the spring and planted and set out on the balcony or patio when all danger of frost has passed.

You have the fun of watching — close up — the first shoots appear, then the breathless sighting of the first flower spike. Summer-blooming bulbs can be bought from mail order catalogues, garden centers and sometimes grocery or department stores, although we recommend you buy them from the first two sources. You do not know what harsh treatment and unfavorable conditions bulbs might have undergone in nongarden stores.

In garden centers you can buy bulbs already potted up for patio or balcony use. They are also sold in clear plastic bags of sphagnum moss, sawdust or peat moss, or in open bins so you can feel and see the condition of the bulbs before you buy them. Do not buy bulbs that are packaged so that you cannot see the bulb itself — no telling what condition it is in.

Buying from reputable mail order firms ensures top-quality bulbs. If the firm is a good one, you can return any damaged or rotten bulbs. Also, mail order catalogues give you a greater choice within each bulb category as well as a wider choice of rarer bulbs.

Check the bulbs to see if any insects have hitched a ride. The most commonly seen bulb pests are aphids. Immediately return any aphid-infested packages. Check also for soft patches, rotten roots, deep cuts and bruises. Be sure bulbs are firm, not spongy or shriveled, and feel heavy for their size. Overly light bulbs have dried out. Select the largest bulbs you can find or afford — larger bulb size usually means more and larger flowers. Also, buy close to the time you plan to plant. If planting time is delayed, be sure you store the bulbs in a dry, cool place with their packages open.

Bulbs thrive in light, well-draining potting mixes in containers that have more than adequate drainage. One small drainage hole will not be sufficient. Enlarge the one hole or create at least four more. Cover the drainage hole with pot shards or a piece of screening. The pot should be deep enough to allow 2 in./5 cm of potting mix below the bulb for good root development. The pot should also be deep enough so that about a 1 in./2.5 cm space is left between the soil line and the rim of the pot, to make watering easier.

Place the flat, knobbly end of the bulb, the end where the roots develop, on the bottom layer of potting mix. Many have an obvious flat end, but some are confusing. If in doubt, lay the bulbs on their sides. A dahlia root is a big ugly sprawl of wrinkled, dried-up potato-looking things. Plant it so that the potatoes stream downwards from their small central knob.

In the pot, allow enough space between bulbs to suit the grown size of whatever you are planting. Twist them in firmly, to ensure solid contact with the potting mix. After placing the bulbs, fill in with potting mix. Most bulbs appreciate 1–2 in./2.5–5 cm of soil over their tops. Water thoroughly. Set outdoors in sun or shade as appropriate, once all danger of frost has passed.

Gardeners with a little extra space indoors often start these plants indoors about three weeks before the last frost date. Just pot up as above and place the pots somewhere indoors, out of the way. If you time it right, the plants will begin to show green just when they can be put outside. This way they will have a head start on the blossoming season, and do not need supplemental indoor grow-lighting.

AUTUMN CARE

Bulbs add variety to the no-garden garden. However, their bloom time, like perennials, is limited. After blooming, you could compost them or throw them out, but a better approach is to give them a little special care so they will be ready to grow again next year.

After they have finished blossoming, allow them to complete their cycle of leaf growth, food storage and bulb ripening by continuing to water them until their leaves turn yellow. Then trim away the above-ground part of the plant and compost it. Dig up the bulbs and let them dry indoors somewhere airy for a few days. Then bury them in an open tray of dry sand or peat moss and store the tray in a dark, dry and cool place. Five to ten degrees above the freezing point, if you can manage it. If not, cool room temperatures are fine. Dryness is more important than temperature, so do not put the bulbs in the fridge, which is too damp. Never seal in a plastic bag, or even a closed paper bag. In spring, plant outdoors as you would new bulbs or start them early indoors — see our instructions above.

The following is a list of commonly available summer-flowering bulbs. Buy them in garden centers or from a good mail order catalogue.

AGAPANTHUS, lily of the Nile, blue African lily, *Agapanthus*

The fleshy roots of this sun-lover send up mounds of strap-like leaves, while rounded clusters of large blue six-petaled flowers are borne on pencil-thick green stems throughout the summer. Height 18–48 in./45–120 cm. These bulbs can be left in the same container year after year (overwinter the pot indoors, water sparingly until new growth resumes). The evergreen dwarf forms respond especially well to container culture. They blossom better when they are root-bound, so do not disturb the plants until they are literally growing out of the pot. However, be sure the container is sturdy, as agapanthus roots can burst clay pots.

ANEMONE, *Anemone*

Anemone blooms in white or shades of pink, red, blue and purple. The flowers are daisy-like, about 2 in./5 cm wide, while the plant's overall height is 6–24 in./15–60 cm. Blossoms in spring, prefers sun or light shade. Plant the claw-shaped tubers 1–2 in./2.5–5 cm below soil level; soak the tubers in tepid water for about 48 hours before planting. The flowers are sun-lovers — they open in sun and close at night or on cloudy days.

CALADIUM, *Caladium*

These bulbs are grown for their magnificent foliage, which persists all summer. Many color combinations can be found: green-veined white-leaved combinations; green-veined red leaves; red-veined silver leaves; red-veined white leaves; multicolored, all-mixed-up leaves; and many others. The leaves are large — usually about 6–10 in./15–25 cm long and arrowhead-shaped. The plant's height is 12–14 in./30–35 cm. Likes partial to full shade and enjoys hot, humid weather. The bulbs should be just covered with potting mix. Three tubers to an 8 in./20 cm diameter pot are usually sufficient to put on a brilliant show. They need depth for root development. They can be effectively grouped with tuberous begonias. One of your authors just loves these gorgeous things but they drive her mad, because hers wind up with great big leaves on skinny little stems that break, so the leaf dies. You can stake the bigger leaves, but the trick is to catch them before the stems break. The best solution is to add to the pot, at planting time, a few branchy twigs to support the leaves as they grow.

DWARF CANNA, *Canna generalis*

Foliage is tropical-looking, broad, 6–12 in./15–30 cm long and can be blue-green, bright green or bronze. Flowers bloom in rich reds, pink, bronze, yellow, and orange as well as bicolors. Overall height is about 30 in./75 cm. Blossom time is mid-August to mid-September; if started indoors early, they may bloom all summer long. Place in sun. Buy only the dwarf varieties; the taller ones grow to 5 ft./1.5 m and are difficult to manage in containers. Plant about 6 in./15 cm below soil level. Remove flowers as they fade and then cut the stem down to soil level when blooming is completed. If stored in a dry, cool place, can be carried through to the next year.

DAHLIA, *Dahlia*

Many types: cactus-flowered, pompoms, doubles, singles. Wide range of exciting colors, except blue. Wonderful dark reds are available. Height is 12–60 in./30–150 cm, depending on the variety. Expect continuous bloom though the summer. Prefers sun, but can stand partial shade. The dwarf varieties are suitable for containers. Some of the larger types are too difficult to wrestle with, although you might try them in a half-barrel. Plant the bulbs about 6 in./15 cm below soil level. Pinch out the center when about six leaves have appeared. If this is repeatedly done, a bushier plant will form. Dahlias are readily available in garden centers and mail order catalogues. In autumn, dig them up after frost nips the leaves, remove the potting mix, then roll them up in newspapers. The storage place must be cool and somewhat moist. If too moist they may rot, if too dry, they may shrivel up. We find that too-dry does less harm than too-moist. 'Patio Baby' dahlias are a favorite container variety. Their bright pink daisy-like flowers are about 2 in./5 cm across and have yellow centers. Watch out for earwigs (the flowers will look tattered and brown) and set nonchemical traps if they appear. Dahlias like a rich soil (lots of compost) and monthly feeding with 10-10-10 fertilizer.

LILY, *Lilium*

Narrow green leaves on thick green stems. Flowers are trumpet-shaped or recurved. Comes in many colors. Height is 18–60 in./45–150 cm, depending on the variety. Blooms spring through summer, depending on the variety. Each variety has a short (not longer than 14 days) bloom time. Grow it in the sun. Lilies like sun on their flowers but shade on their roots. Choose the low growers, such as dwarf Oriental lilies, which are under 24 in./60 cm, and put them in 18 in./45 cm tall pots. Cover the bulb with about 5 in./12 cm of potting mix. Sometimes you can find lilies already potted up in garden centers. It can be argued that lilies are better in pots than in beds, because many of them have the infuriating habit of looking dreadful the moment they finish flowering, leaving a nasty brown spot in the middle of the bed. In the container garden, browned-off potted lilies can be hidden while they finish browning off (they are busy storing up food in their roots, ready for next year), at which point they can be unearthed and dried, ready for winter storage.

RANUNCULUS, Persian buttercup, *Ranunculus*

Blooms for about six weeks in a good year, late spring into early summer. Flowers are shades of red, pink, yellow, orange, white. Related to the buttercup. Height is 10–24 in./25–60 cm. Place in sun. Does well in pots. Soak the tuber for a few hours before planting it with the claw facing down. Cover with 1 in./2.5 cm of potting mix. Likes moist soil, good drainage and cool weather, so do not place it in hot spots such as close to a masonry wall.

TIGRIDIA, tigerflower, shellflower, *Tigridia*

Large, flamboyant three-petaled flowers (6 in./15 cm) in red, pink, yellow, orange, white, bicolors. Centers are often speckled. Height is 18–30 in./45–75 cm. Bloom time covers July into August. Plant bulbs in succession for a longer period of flower, in sun, although it can stand some shade. Very showy, so be careful what they rub shoulders with — they will shout down humbler flowers. Good for cutting, though each blossom lasts only a day. Sometimes known as Mexican shell flower.

TUBEROUS BEGONIA, *Begonia tuberhybrida*

Big, bright green, asymmetrical arrowhead-shaped leaves on fleshy stalks. Flowers (summer through fall) come in different forms and many shades of red, pink, yellow, orange, white, also picotee; usually doubles. Some have big flowers, some small. Some are magnificent, rose-blossom-shaped flowers that measure nearly 6 in./15 cm across. Pendulous versions can be found in bulb catalogues. Not all that tall: 12–20 in./30–50 cm. Tends to grow rather wide — as much as 24 in./60 cm.

Plant tubers indoors (provide artificial light as soon as they show green) a couple of months before the last frost to prolong the blooming season. This is one of the few tubers to bloom throughout the season. Grow on in partial shade; plants become leggy if put in too dense shade. They can develop mildew from inadequate air circulation. Keep soil evenly moist — never, but never, let it dry out or stay soggy. The potting mix should cover the bulbs only to a depth of half an inch/1 cm. Sometimes the larger-flowered varieties need to be staked because the weight of the flowers pulls the branches down. Some authorities say that when the tubers sprout, you should pinch off all but the three most vigorous shoots to promote a bushier plant. Brittle stems, so do not bump it. Treat it right and it will last for years, so do not be afraid to spend a little money on a special tuber you really love.

MIX AND MATCH

Bulbs and tubers take a little extra work because they need to be overwintered in the proper circumstances, but they repay this effort by hanging around several years. If you like the idea of finding precisely the right color to suit your exacting tastes, begonias and dahlias in particular are for you. They both have big fan clubs, which means the breeders have been hybridizing a vast selection of flower colors and forms. Hunt hard enough and you will be able to find one that precisely matches . . . the upholstery of your outdoor chairs, the bridesmaids' gowns for a very special garden wedding, the shade of pink that most flatters your skin . . . but not, alas, your baby blue eyes. Hybridizers have not broken the blue barrier in these two bulb families.

Chapter 14

Moveable Feasts:

Herbs and Vegetables

....

HERBS IN POTS

Herbs are a boon to the container gardener because most of them are perfectly happy to grow on the dry side. We like to have a selection growing close to the kitchen door, since it is so satisfying to dart outside for a little sprig of something fresh for the soup.

Mind you, not every herb is a brilliant wonder to behold. On the contrary, most herbs are fairly humble-looking plants. Yet they make good foils for flashier plants. Most of them will, when planted with annuals, repel one or more insect pests. Most parts of herb plants are aromatic. One of us once grew chamomile, which escaped into the lawn, so now every time she mows over that area she is rewarded for her labors with a nice waft of chamomile scent.

It is quite possible to grow nothing but herbs and still have an attractive garden. The range of leaf textures and colors, heights and widths can be mixed into an artistic grouping. Flower colors are usually yellow, white, lavender or pink. Herbs mix well into displays of brighter-colored annuals and vegetables.

Harvesting your herb crop in fall will provide fragrant summer memories in each winter meal. Dry or freeze the usable parts (listed with each herb below). To dry herbs, simply lay them out in a shallow layer on paper or cloth towels on a cookie sheet. Place them out of direct sun, but where the air is dry. Turn them now and then, until they are thoroughly dried out. Crumble into a tight-lidded jar and use as needed.

The culinary herbs listed below are safe to eat, of course, but only if they are not contaminated by herbicides or pesticides. Herb plants purchased in garden centers sometimes have been sprayed. Be sure to thoroughly wash the leaves before using in your favorite dishes. We ourselves are organic gardeners and strongly urge you never to use toxic chemicals.

GROWING AND MAINTAINING HERBS

Herbs, despite their general willingness to grow happily for you, do ask for a potting mix high in organic material. We often plant ours in pots filled exclusively with compost —

home-made if we have some, otherwise store-bought. Well-rotted manure purchased in bags at the garden center works well, too. Good drainage is essential, for soggy roots will quickly lead to weak, unhealthy plants. If your herbs threaten to become leggy, pinch out their top-most growing tips to encourage bushiness and to direct growing energy into making leaves. Do not buy herbs in flower — the flowers use up energy and food better directed into the leaves. Buy stocky, bushy plants that are solid in their containers. Keep the new transplants sheltered from sun and wind for the first few days until they become established. Most require sunny locations. If you choose to grow herbs from seed, sow the seeds directly into the pots they will grow in. Remember, you can eat the thinnings.

HERBS IN AUTUMN

Some herbs are annuals and are gone forever every autumn when the frost kills them. Some are perennials but will not survive the winter outdoors if left in above-ground pots (see Appendix I). Either way, container gardeners have two options: take the pots indoors and overwinter them as houseplants, to have ready to plant out again in spring, or start anew each year from purchased plants or seeds.

If you have an in-ground bed, you can grow perennial herbs (noted below) as you would other perennials.

SPECIAL CHARACTERISTICS

Chervil, chamomile, fennel and mint are said to attract

beneficial insects, while chives, coriander, dill, fennel, mint, parsley, sage, sweet marjoram, summer savory and thyme are said to repel the harmful ones. Bees and butterflies are attracted by mint, rosemary, sage, sweet marjoram, summer savory and thyme.

Catnip (*Nepeta cataria*) is a herb sometimes grown to repel insects. We recommend that you not grow it in the open garden, because every cat in the neighborhood will come to visit. One of us does, however, grow a pot of catnip wa-a-a-a-y up high on an indoor shelf that none of her cats can reach, not even the young, agile one.

OUR LIST OF HERBS

BALM, lemon balm, *Melissa officinalis*

Attracts bees. Lemony-flavored leaves used in desserts, fish, stuffing and drinks. Sedative tea. Height is 18–24 in./45–60 cm, spreads to half that. Seeds take a long time to germinate, but once growing the plants spread rapidly. Perennial.

BASIL, *Ocimum basilicum*

Said to repel mosquitoes. Leaves used in stews, tomato sauces and other savory dishes. And, of course, pesto, yum. Pinch off flower buds to keep leaves coming and to prevent legginess. Decorative purple-leaved, ruffled-leaved and lemon-scented varieties. Some grow as tall as 24 in./60 cm, but most are shorter. Spreads to about its own height, maybe a bit less. Annual.

BAY, bay laurel, *Laurus nobilis*

Leaves used in many savory dishes, especially stews and soups, but remove them before serving because they are too tough to eat. This large shrub or small tree is not suitable for growing in cold-winter areas unless you have a large indoor space and high indoor light levels. Grows to 40 ft./13 m in its natural habitat, but can be kept pruned to 6 ft./2 m.

CHAMOMILE, *Matricaria chamomilla*

Small, pretty daisy-like flowers. Foliage is very attractive — fine and ferny. Fresh or dried flowers are used to make soothing tea. Height is 6–12 in./15–30 cm. Fine in hot areas. Perennial.

CHERVIL, *Anthriscus cerefolium*

Small white flowers, bright green fern-like leaves. Leaves taste a little like anise (licorice) and are used in fruit salads and savory dishes. Pinch out flower buds, or it will become leggy and sparse. Seeds germinate quickly, so can make successive sowings over the summer. Water well. Grows about 24 in./60 cm tall. Annual.

CHIVES, *Allium schoenoprasum*

Member of the onion family. Leaves used in salads, cold dishes. Attractive balls of purple or pink flowers. Height is 12 in./30 cm. Also garlic chive, a little taller and with white flowers. Perennial.

CORIANDER, cilantro, *Coriandrum sativum*

Do not remove coriander's white flowers because the seeds are a main reason you grow it. The ground seeds and chopped leaves are a mainstay of Indian cuisine. In Mexican cuisine the leaves are called cilantro. Plant resembles parsley. Height is 18 in./45 cm. Annual.

DILL, *Anethum graveolens*

Attracts bees when yellow flowers, which look like Queen Anne's lace, open. Can sprawl a lot, so will need support in the pot. Both leaves and seeds (do not disbud) used to flavor many dishes. Height is 36 in./90 cm or more. Water well. Annual.

FENNEL, *Foeniculum vulgare*

This is a big plant, 36–48 in./90–120 cm tall. Looks a lot like dill, with its airy, feathery leaves. Anise flavor (licorice). Use seeds or chopped leaves (freeze or dry them for winter) with fish, pork, veal, soups. Some varieties have a bulbous base that is eaten as a vegetable. Perennial.

MARJORAM, POT, *Origanum onites*

Long stems bear mauve flowers. Whole plant is scented. Leaves flavor savory dishes. Height is 12 in./30 cm. Perennial.

MARJORAM, SWEET, *Origanum majorana*

Fragrant plant. Gray leaves. Use in savory dishes, salads. Remove flower buds to encourage leaves. Height is 24 in./60 cm. Perennial.

MINT, *Mentha*

Several types are available in garden centers and seed catalogues: apple, peppermint, spearmint. Thank goodness container gardeners do not have the same worry that in-ground gardeners have with this vigorous perennial: given half a chance mint, no matter which variety, could take over the world. Pinch out the insignificant flowers to encourage more leaves. Tea is said to cure headaches. Use leaves for mint sauce, jelly, to flavor lamb dishes. Likes a little shade. Height is 24–36 in./60–90 cm. Perennial.

OREGANO, *Origanum vulgare*

A sprawly plant, only one is needed per pot. Use in savory dishes, especially tomato sauces. Height is 24 in./60 cm tall. Perennial.

PARSLEY, *Petroselinum crispum*

Chew the leaves to remove liquor, garlic and onions from your breath. Some varieties have curly leaves, some are flatter. Use in savory dishes and as a garnish. Height is 12 in./30 cm. Biennial.

ROSEMARY, *Rosmarinus officinalis*

One of us has now brought a rosemary plant through two winters (outdoors in summer, indoors under lights in winter) and thinks it looks very handsome sitting on the corner of the patio keeping company with two pink geraniums. Use the chopped leaves sparingly on savory dishes — too much and the food tastes like a pine tree. You can make soothing tea, but we have never tried it, because of the pine tree thing. Said to repel slugs, snails, other insects. Large, slow-growing plant. Plant one or two per 12 in./30 cm pot. Can grow to be a sizable shrub (6 ft./2 m) in warmer climates, but if grown in a pot will not get much taller than 24–36 in./60–90 cm. Cut back by about half in fall.

SAGE, *Salvia officinalis*

A nice little gray-leaved plant often grown as an ornamental. Purple, yellow or white-variegated types also available. Rough-textured leaves used in savory dishes. Needs growing points pinched out regularly to encourage bushiness. Height is 24 in./60 cm. Perennial, if protected.

SAVORY, SUMMER, *Satureja hortensis*

Tiny shiny green leaves. The taste of the leaf is peppery-minty. For best flavor, harvest leaves before the insignificant lavender or pink flowers appear. Good with beans, meat, soup, stew, fish, salads. Steep to make a tea. Height is 15 in./40 cm, spreads to half its height. Annual.

SAVORY, WINTER, *Satureja montana*

Use in the same dishes as summer savory, although it has a more bitter taste. We hear that dried winter savory mixed with dried basil is an acceptable salt substitute. Height is 6–12 in./15–30 cm, spreads to one and a half times that. Perennial.

TARRAGON (French), *Artemisia dracunculas sativa*

French tarragon is the proper one for culinary use. It will not grow from seeds, so you must buy plants. Russian tarragon (*A. dracunculoides*) does grow from seed, but has an inferior flavor. Use leaves in savory dishes. Height is 24–36 in./60–90 cm. Perennial.

THYME, English thyme, common thyme, *Thymus vulgaris*

Leaves widely used in meat, fish, vegetable dishes. Height is 12 in./30 cm, spreads about the same. There is also lemon thyme, *T. serpyllum* or *T. citriodorus*, used the same way if you fancy the slight lemon tang it adds. Creeping thyme, *T. praecox*, can be planted between paving stones. Perennial.

VERBENA, LEMON, *Lippia citriodora*

Long narrow leaves used in teas and fruit salad. Needs to be sheltered from wind. In natural habitat, grows to 5 ft./1.5 m. Perennial in milder climates.

VEGETABLES IN POTS

For some of us, there is nothing so tasty as a sun-ripened tomato we have grown ourselves. Although many of us do not have the land to fully indulge our vegetable fantasies, this does not have to deter intrepid no-garden vegetable growers. Carrots can be grown on the window sill, baskets of radishes can be hung from the porch eaves, and bean vines can be trained around the balcony railings.

The secret to successful crops? At least six hours of sun a day, a good measure of soil (as against nonsoil elements such as perlite) in the potting mix and deep containers for large plants and root crops. The ability to think vertical also helps, because balcony or patio vegetable growers need to cleverly use all available space.

SUNNY ENOUGH FOR YOU?

Before you buy a pair of overalls and a pitchfork, first find out whether your space gets the required sun. If the area has a southern or western exposure, without shadows from nearby buildings, trees or fences, you should be able to grow vegetables successfully. If your space has an eastern exposure, you will be limited to maybe lettuce and some root vegetables. Northern exposures present challenges and pretty much limit your crops to radishes and lettuce. If you are not sure, pick a sunny day and go out and see if your growing area has direct sun at 8 am, 10 am, 12 noon, 2 pm and 4 pm. Add up the hours of direct sun. Six and over, haul out the hoe. Under four and you had best buy your produce.

SOIL

Vegetable potting mixes need to be richer than ones used for ornamentals — veggies are heavy feeders. This means more soil in the mix, which makes the mix heavier. Balcony gardeners will not want to overdo this. A good combination is a commercial potting mix augmented with vermiculite and commercial topsoil, compost or well-rotted manure.

Planting your vegetables just in topsoil is not a good idea. For one thing, it will be too heavy and for another, topsoil in small containers has a tendency to compact. This means that water will not penetrate as well and root growth will be stunted.

POTS, POLES AND POSTS

You can use the same type of containers for vegetables as you use for ornamentals. Be inventive and use many types of "found" containers. Just be sure that each has at least one drainage hole — large containers will need more. Some vegetables can be grown in quite a small pot, say, 4 in./10 cm, but please be sure to read about watering in Chapter 12. Root vegetables, such as carrots, need deep pots — 12 in./30 cm.

To increase the number of vegetable pots in your space, think vertically:

- Attach hooks for hanging baskets to the ceiling beams of your porch.
- Increase the space available on balcony, deck or patio with brick and board shelves or even a simple board and sawhorse arrangement.
- Grow climbing vegetables such as beans, peas and viney tomato varieties such as 'Sweet 100.'
- Train plants up commercial trellises or up strings attached from pot to ceiling, against walls, or from railing to ceiling.
- Make teepee frames of poles and use them to grow viney veggies such as beans. You can make a teepee with each

pole in a pot, a bean plant trained up each leg. If you push the poles (pots) close together this arrangement takes up only 24 in. x 24 in./60 cm x 60 cm.

• See Chapter 4 where we describe hanging frames and other apparatus that can be pressed into service for vegetable growing.

TO SEED OR NOT TO SEED

If you are an enthusiastic, experienced gardener, you may want to start your plants from seed. This, in a cold-winter climate, will have to be done indoors. Start most seeds at least a month before the date you can set them outdoors. You will need a sterile potting mix to prevent "damping off," a fungal disease that kills seedlings. Use shallow trays that fit easily on a window sill or under grow-lights. Seedlings need strong sunlight at least six hours a day for optimum growth. Follow package directions for proper planting depths. Remember to water, but not drown. Too wet a mix can cause damping off. Turn window sill seedlings daily or they will grow with a permanent lean towards the light.

If you want the largest possible selection of varieties, buy seeds from the catalogues. If not, check out the display at the garden center. Potted plants found in garden centers are the smallest selection, but you cannot beat their convenience.

When choosing the varieties you want to grow, read the descriptions carefully. Discount the praise given to each — all catalogue descriptions of flavor and appearance make the variety sound like the best thing since sliced bread. Rather, make your choice based on the days to maturity — choose the earliest. Next, consider whether you want to grow a dwarf or midget variety — the easiest to deal with in limited-space gardens. Some vegetables, such as cucumbers and tomatoes, have been specifically bred for patio and container culture. Choose these. For example, a favorite cucumber for container growing is 'Patio Pik.'

If you are not interested in cluttering up the window sills with seed flats, then consider buying seedlings and plants from your local garden center. You can usually find Boston lettuce, Romaine lettuce, cherry tomatoes, bush tomatoes, cucumbers, eggplants, broccoli and so on in flats. These have to be transplanted into larger containers and spaced properly. You can also buy onion seedlings, but we have found it faster to grow onions from "sets," or onion bulbs. Some garden centers also offer tomato plants, and some other vegetables, already grown well on to maturity in large pots. These are usually labelled "patio tomatoes." All you have to do is take the pot home and put a saucer under it.

When you buy plants, check them thoroughly for signs of insect or disease infestations. Look suspiciously at the leaves' undersides. Jostle the plant and take a close-up squint at the soil — anything with legs in there? Do not buy plants that are yellow-looking and spindly. Buy those that have a strong color, a firm stem and are bushy. As an extra precaution, when you bring the plants home, wash them down.

Maintain the same degree of watchfulness, plant hygiene and care for your vegetables as for your other plants. Do not let vegetable containers dry out until the plants wilt. The growing season is short, and any stress just postpones harvest time. Fertilize as you would ornamentals — every two or three weeks, regularly.

If you notice an insect infestation, do not use chemical sprays — remember you want to eat these plants. Use a soap-and-water, garlic-and-water or hot-pepper-and-water spray that can be easily washed off at harvest. Please see Chapter 15 on bugs and diseases.

DOWN TO SPECIFICS

Your authors have grown an assortment of vegetables in pots over the years and a season never passes when they do not have a tomato or two in a pot. We suggest a salad garden — lettuce, tomatoes, onions and radishes. Enthusiasts can add beans, cucumbers and carrots.

If growing from seed, you can plant succession crops: plant the first few pots of, say, lettuce. Then wait two weeks to plant the second batch of lettuce seeds. Extending the harvest time this way works for many vegetables except tomatoes, which need as long a season as possible.

We recommend the following vegetables for small-space, no-garden gardens.

BEANS

Whether you want string beans or lima beans, you can choose between bush types and pole types. Bush beans can be grown in pots without supports, while pole beans need a support. Bush varieties grow about 20 in./50 cm tall, and pole beans can reach at least 8 ft./2.4 m. Beans are rarely offered in preplanted flats, so you must start them from seeds. If you grow bush beans, space them about 3 in./8 cm apart in a container at least 8 in./20 cm deep. Pole beans need the same depth of pot. All varieties need full sun. Remember to keep the beans picked to encourage the plant to produce more. Do not let the beans ripen until they are bulging and huge — they taste woody. 'Scarlet Runner' (see Chapter 12 for fuller description) is an old-fashioned pole bean that climbs vigorously up any support. Its bright red flowers are quite ornamental. However, the beans must be picked and eaten young for the best flavor and texture. Teeny little beans in a salad are a treat that nongardeners never get to enjoy.

CARROTS

You usually have to start these from seeds — garden centers rarely offer carrots in flats because they (the carrots, not the garden centers) do not enjoy transplanting. The good news is that there is a huge variety of seeds to choose from. Follow planting depth directions on the packet. Thin after sprouting to about 2 in./5 cm apart. Thin again whenever they look crowded — these thinnings (tiny carrots) are great in salads. The depth of the container will depend on the variety of carrot. Obviously the long varieties, which can grow to almost 10 in./25 cm, will need a container at least 12 in./30 cm deep. 'Thumbelina,' a small round carrot, can grow to the size of a golfball — it is especially good for containers. 'Minicor' grows 3–5 in./8–13 cm long and is also adaptable to container culture. Whichever varieties you choose, you can plant a second batch two weeks after the first to extend the harvest. The ferny tops of carrots are pretty and are good for interplanting with flowers. Do not let the soil dry out too often, or the carrots will crack. Can take some shade.

CUCUMBER

Cucumbers are long, viney plants, good for hanging baskets, trellises or posts. Choose varieties bred specifically for small-space gardens. Grow them from seed or in preplanted pots from garden centers. Plant seeds about 6 in./15 cm apart in 5 gal./20 L or larger containers. This size can support two or three plants. Cucumbers are heavy feeders, so fertilize often and never let the plants dry out. They need sunny locations. Keep picking cucumbers as they ripen to encourage more fruit. Also pick them before they turn yellow — they taste bitter the older they get. A new patio container variety is 'Salad Bush,' which spreads only about 3 ft./1 m.

LETTUCE

Most varieties of lettuce are extremely easy to grow. They grow happily in small or large containers and need less sunlight than other vegetables. The fastest-growing are the loose-leaf varieties, followed by Boston and Romaine types. Head lettuce, the type you buy at the grocery store, takes nearly an entire summer to mature. Grow from seed or buy flats of different varieties at the garden center. Lettuce prefers cool weather, so start early — around the same time you plant spinach. Plant about 10 in./25 cm apart in large containers, if you plan to harvest the outer leaves as they mature. If you plan to harvest the entire plant at once, plant 4 in./10 cm apart. To lengthen the crop season, plant seeds at two week intervals. Thinnings can be eaten. Lettuce grows rapidly, so do not forget to feed the plants. Hungry lettuce leaves turn yellow.

ONIONS

Onions are easily grown from sets, or bulbs. Plant them about 2 in./5 cm apart in 12 in./30 cm deep pots. Onions are moisture-lovers, so do not let the soil dry out, but do not keep it wringing wet either or the bulbs may rot. They also like cool weather, so start them outdoors earlier than other crops. You can plant onion bulbs close together and use the thinnings in salads. As onions mature, their tops will yellow and fall over, a sign that the bulb is growing, on its way to becoming a cooking onion. Some people bend the tops over to encourage this. Trim off any seed heads that form. When harvesting, if the soil mix is loose enough, you can pull the bulbs out. If there is any resistance, dig them out with a kitchen spoon. Onions can take some shade.

RADISH

These are the favorite vegetables of many primary school science teachers. Radishes are early to mature and nearly foolproof to grow. You can pick from many varieties and colors. Grow from seed; they are rarely offered in flats. Plant the seeds about 1 in./2.5 cm apart in a container 4–8 in./10–20 cm deep, depending on the variety grown. Radishes like cool weather and can be planted at the same time as onions. Extremely "hot" radishes have come from containers where the soil was allowed to dry out once too often. Also, radishes grown in the hottest time of the summer tend to be pithy. Pick your radishes when they are about the size of a jawbreaker. As they grow larger, they become woody. Radishes can be grown in light shade with some periods of sun.

SPINACH

Spinach is a fast-growing plant that prefers the cool weather of spring and early fall. Grow from seed in 4 in./10 cm pots and thin to about 2 in./5 cm apart. Spinach is a good vegetable for successive sowings — plant at about ten-day intervals. Pinch out the flower bud as soon as it appears because spinach will go to seed rapidly and stop producing leaves. Keep the soil moist and fertilize often. Spinach grows best in full sun. Swiss chard is similar, and will withstand a few frosts.

TOMATO

Tomatoes luxuriate in heat and sun. They can be started from seed, but why not get a head start and buy them in pots? You can choose standard or small (cherry) tomatoes. The larger varieties and vine types need to be staked in the pot or given some form of support. When in fruit, the branches become heavy and could break. Small varieties such as 'Tiny Tim' can be grown in a 4 in./10 cm diameter pot. Patio hybrids are often grown in 12 in./30 cm diameter pots. Standard bush tomato plants need at least a 5 gal./20 L size. If you grow them in a window box or other large container, be sure they are spaced at least 12 in./30 cm apart.

Tomato stems are unusual in that they will sprout roots when covered with soil. Experienced gardeners capitalize on this by planting seedlings at a depth that covers up to one half the length of the stem. This makes the plants grow more compactly. As the plant matures, pinch out the small shoots that appear where branches meet the main stem. These shoots can produce lots of leaves and take energy away from flower production and, thus, fruit setting. Do not let the soil dry out — this can cause rot to form on the tomato. On the other hand, excessive watering increases the size of the tomato but diminishes the flavor.

COME AND EAT

You probably will not harvest enough from your pots to fill the freezer and feed a family of ten for the winter, but you will get enough to brighten meals during the summer and autumn. And always remember that vegetables and flowers can be planted in together (see our plant combination suggestions in Chapter 2). Just bear in mind their cultural needs.

Chapter 15

They Know Where You Live:

Insects, Diseases, and Weeds

....

Insects, plant diseases and weeds are always with us. "I beg your pardon," you say, "I live on the twenty-first floor in the middle of a concrete jungle. How would such pests ever find my plants?"

Easy. Remember the flat of marigolds you just bought? Well, lurking beneath the leaves and in the soil were some destructive pests who hitchhiked a ride into your balcony garden, just thirsting for fresh material to devour. This is one of the reasons you absolutely must inspect any plants you plan to buy before bringing them home. To better your chances of having a bug-free summer, rinse newly purchased plants — soil and all — in a bucket of 40 parts water to 1 part liquid dishsoap (not detergent). Make sure all surfaces are washed. Then rinse them all in fresh water.

No matter how carefully you wash and watch, Mother Nature can still outwit you. Insects and disease also hitchhike into your garden on your clothes, on your pets and on the wind. Weeds can find your address by floating their seeds on an updraft. More often, weeds are waiting in unsterilized potting mixes, rather like a bunch of Sleeping Uglies waiting for Prince Charming (you, with your kindly watering and other care) to come along and give them the kiss of life.

The answer? Deal with each threat as you find it. Once pests have taken hold, it will be a fight to the death — theirs or your plant's. Constant watchfulness for insects, diseases and weeds must become part of your maintenance chores. As you cruise through your outdoor collection on your way to the hammock, or while you're watering, get into the habit of taking a moment to check the stems, the undersides of leaves and the axil (the point where leaf joins stem) for insects. Note if anything flies away or falls from the plant when you jostle it or if there are any strange new inhabitants scurrying around in the pot. Leaves changing color? Could be a sign of disease.

PREVENTION

Prevention is always better than treatment. The main thing is to practice proper plant hygiene:

- Keep the growing area free of dead leaves.
- Allow good air circulation.

- Water regularly.

- Fertilize regularly.

- Wash plants occasionally.

If you do notice a plant in distress, isolate it immediately. You want to contain the damage before it spreads throughout your entire collection. This will give you time to accurately identify what is wrong — disease, insect, soil deficiency or faulty maintenance.

KNOW WHEN TO QUIT

A piece of old-timers' advice: in our short growing season, it is not worthwhile to nurse a sick pot of annuals. By the time you have eliminated a severe infestation, summer is generally over. The best solution for a badly infested pot of annuals is to put the plant in the garbage (not the composter) and replace it. Give the pot a thorough wash before reusing it.

NO NUKES

We would like to discourage the all-out-warfare use of heavy-duty chemicals to eradicate bugs. Remember that they kill the many beneficial bugs (bees, ladybugs and so on) along with the baddies. So many hideous side effects, both personal and environmental, are attached to these compounds, they are not worth the risk. And remember that you are working in a small area, so all the nasty warnings about their risks goes double. In our container gardens, we use nothing stronger than plain old soft dishsoap or insecticidal soap, and our plants have not been overrun by nasty lifeforms.

Your first and best approach to garden pests is prevention, which means good gardening. If your plants have proper light, moisture and food, they will be healthy, and a healthy plant resists pests, which like hyenas, prey primarily on the weak.

BENEFICIAL BUGS

Please note that not all bugs are plant-eating horrors. An effective means of insect control uses the killing instincts of beneficial insects, such as dragonflies, which eat mosquito larvae, or the well-loved ladybug, which eats aphids for breakfast, lunch and dinner. If you see a ladybug sitting around looking bored, gently pick her up and carry her to a favorite container plant and let her feast on any hidden aphids. Damselflies and spiders are also great insect eaters, as are a number of wasps. Hornets are beneficial because they eat many caterpillars, but unfortunately their sting does not feel so beneficial. We realize you may not welcome introducing an insect menagerie onto your balcony or deck — so practice preventive maintenance.

Sometimes worms find their way into containers. If so, be glad, for they are hard at work improving the soil. Top-dress with a little compost, to give them something to work with.

And now, sigh, back to the . . .

BAD BUGS: A ROGUES' GALLERY

Insects love to feast on container plants. The plants are gourmet oases where hungry bugs find self-serve, all-you-can-eat havens. In general, your first weapon against insects is a blast of water from the hose. Not strong enough to explode the plant into a million pieces or wash all the soil out of the pot, but strong enough to knock the pests off the plant and make them decide to move next door. If that fails, spray the infected plant with a solution of water and soap, mixed 40 parts to 1. Sometimes simply cutting off the infested part of the plant is enough.

Aphid

Aphids

One of the most common container plant pests is the aphid. Usually the aphids you will see are soft-bodied, tiny and green.

Aphids cluster in large groups on buds and on new plant growth, sucking out plant fluids, stunting and finally killing the plant. They leave a sticky trail behind them, called honeydew. Besides sticky leaves, other signs of aphid infestation include yellowing leaves, deformed leaves and flowers, and sickly buds that usually drop off or turn yellow. Lady aphids can give birth to hundreds of babies every ten days without any assistance from a male. Why aren't we knee-deep in the little critters? Birds and ladybugs love to eat aphids. Unhappily, birds and ladybugs mainly hunt in the natural garden rather than the container garden. So you must often take matters in your own hands and squish aphids to death, cut off damaged plant tips, or blast them with a soap-and-water solution.

Caterpillars

Caterpillars of all types and sizes can be carried in on the wind, when young, or can be brought in on other plants. These adolescent forms of moths and butterflies eat large holes in leaves. Some can completely defoliate a plant overnight.

Caterpillar damage can be identified by the ragged, nibbled appearance of affected leaves. They also leave dark specks of excrement on the leaves. Nice, huh? When you notice this, immediately begin a close inspection, using a magnifying glass if necessary, of the damaged plant — stem, both sides of leaves, soil surface. Pick the pesky varmint off your plant and destroy it any way you please. Keep checking the plant for the next few weeks to see if the caterpillar brought any unannounced friends or relatives with it.

Cutworms

A common caterpillar, the cutworm (we *hate* cutworms) lives below the surface of the soil during the day, emerging at night to feed on plant stems until the stems fall over, or look "cut." If you see such damage, poke around in the first 1 in./2.5 cm of soil for the gray-white caterpillar and squash it. Tender young shoots are especially vulnerable.

Cyclamen Mites

The cyclamen mite is just as destructive as its relative the spider mite. You cannot see this tiny predator, only signs of its destruction — stunted, curled and unhealthy-looking leaves. It is extremely difficult to eradicate. Try spraying with the soap-and-water solution.

Earwigs

Small, narrow, brown, with a pair of curved pincers on the back end of their hard-cased bodies, earwigs are a persistent pest. (We *hate* earwigs, too.) They eat everything, and are difficult to control, because they have no fixed address and roam at will, eating everything in their path. They appear in cycles, usually one bad year and three not-so-bad years.

They can be especially destructive in container gardens. Signs of their presence are holes in leaves and flowers, or if allowed to have their way, a completely denuded plant. In the traditional garden, they roam from area to area, but in the container garden, they have a tendency to set up permanent housekeeping. When you fear earwigs have zeroed in on your favorite plant, make the usual check of leaves and stems, and then, if the pot is not too heavy, lift it and look under it and under the saucer. Earwigs like close, damp, dark places to rest after their nightly feasting. Hand pick them and drop into a jar of hot or soapy water or take out your aggressions and stomp them to death. Fortunately, they are not bright and can be trapped: leave 12 in./30 cm lengths of hose or bamboo lying around all night — earwigs will hole up in them at dawn. In the morning shake them into a bucket of hot or soapy water.

Fungus Gnats

Fungus gnats can plague the container garden. When you see these little black flies hovering around your plant, sigh with despair. The flies are the adult, nondestructive, form. The immature stage — thread-like, pale white, difficult-to-find worms — is the main menace. They munch on roots, especially tender root hairs. Their eating habits obviously limit the plant's ability to ingest water and nutrients. The first sign of infestation is usually yellowing leaves. You definitely know you are in trouble when the plant falls over. By then it is too late.

They are usually brought in in soil and especially love overly moist soil conditions. If noticed early on, one of the best methods to destroy them is to let the soil dry out.

Leaf Bugs

Plant or leaf bugs, such as the four-lined bug, harlequin bug, tarnished plant bug and various other bugs, eat ragged holes in a wide variety of plants. Be sure the bug you are planning to murder, however, is actually eating the plant. We remind you that sometimes good bugs are difficult to distinguish from the bad.

Leafhoppers

Leafhoppers, small and green, feed on developing flower and leaf buds. They are difficult to see, but when you brush against plant leaves, they hop mightily. A soap-and-water spray usually eliminates them.

Leaf Miners

Leaf miners are larval forms of a variety of insects. The larvae immediately tunnel into leaves once they hatch out of the egg. The miners eat their way through between the upper and lower surfaces of the leaf. Their presence is signalled by the visible white trails in leaves, a delicate tracery of their internal travels. Less energetic species of leaf miners prefer to hollow out large rooms in one place. It is best to cut off the leaves and throw them in the garbage.

Mealy Bugs

Mealy bugs look like harmless dots of cotton wool decorating stems, leaves and leaf axils. However, these decorative bits of fluff are actually sucking the life fluids out of your plants. They must be dealt with as soon as they appear. Mealy bugs are difficult to eradicate, but try wiping them away with a cotton swab dipped in isopropyl alcohol. It is effective only if you touch each bug with this lethal swab. We also advise you to rub the area down afterwards with the alcohol swab.

Scale

Scale is what it sounds like — a brown oval insect that looks like a hard, brown scale or barnacle attached to a stem or leaf. Scale insects are quite mobile and move from place to place on a plant, hunkering down to suck the life fluids out of any tasty morsel they come across. Scale insects are specialized. Some want to savour only orchid leaves, others like woody ornamentals. They are so tough they can even infest oleander, which is hideously poisonous to most life forms. Scale, with difficulty, can be controlled by rubbing them with isopropyl alcohol. Some are so attached to their host that the only way to remove them is to scrape them off with a fingernail or a dull knife. After removing them, rub the area with the alcohol.

Slugs

Slugs — yuck — are repulsive mobile gray blobs that leave slimy trails behind them. They are night feeders who enjoy most plants. Even if you are way up on a balcony, they might be brought in on other plants. They are less of a pest on decks and patios because they do not like to drag their soft, easily damaged bodies over these rough surfaces. Spread crushed egg shells or sharp sand over the soil as a deterrent. If you sprinkle salt directly on the slugs, they shrivel right up.

Spider Mites

Spider mites, or red spider mites, the bane of the indoor gardener, are also a persistent outdoor container plant pest. Mites are nearly microscopic, but the observant gardener knows to look on the underside of leaves and at the join of leaf to stem for the mite's delicate webbing. They can also be detected by the presence of tiny holes in the plant leaves. If mites are allowed to settle in, affected leaves will turn yellow and drop off. If immediate steps are not taken, mites can multiply rapidly and turn a healthy plant into a defoliated, stunted, web-covered mess. One of your authors lost a lush fuchsia to mites this summer — the first time she had this problem. It was the usual story: the mites got a foothold, the gardener was away, she returned to a *fait accompli*. If you begin spraying in time, insecticidal soap or a garlic-and-water spray usually deals effectively with them.

Thrips

Thrips are so small you do not know they are hiding between petals and in the folds of leaves until you see the damage. They feast on new shoots and developing buds of many plants, especially day lilies and gladioli. Their gourmandizing causes dirty brown or silver streaks on leaves and flowers. Another small destroyer is the *springtail*. It eats tiny holes in leaves, which eventually can stress a plant to the point of death. Their spread is encouraged by overly moist soil.

Whitefly

Whitefly, a small white fly, is the scourge of greenhouse and indoor plants. If you shake a plant and a small white cloud drifts away from the leaves, your plants have whitefly. It multiplies rapidly and can wreak havoc in the garden when they escape outdoors in the summer — luckily they cannot overwinter outdoors. They usually feed on the undersides of leaves, and seem to enjoy a wide variety of container plants, such as fuchsia. Whitefly also like vegetable plants, such as tomatoes.

Sometimes a blast of cold water will take care of them. If you want to be really sure they are being eradicated, attract them to their favorite color, yellow. We have heard of gardeners greasing a small yellow plastic bowl with petroleum jelly or motor oil and placing it near the infected plant. The whiteflies land on the grease, are stuck and eventually die. Other gardeners grease a piece of heavy yellow paper and do the same.

This autumn one of us had an infested fuchsia sitting on the front step for a few nights as she nervously watched the thermometer. She was very lucky, and was able to whisk the plant back indoors after the cold had killed the whitefly but before it killed the fuchsia. This approach often works with cold-sensitive pests, but is risky.

MORE BAD NEWS: DISEASES

Not only insects damage your plants. Plants are also brought low by a variety of fungal (the most common in container gardens), bacterial and viral diseases.

Plant diseases can be signaled by discolorations, spots, rusty blotches, white or gray furry patches, black sooty spots, rotting growth on leaves and stems. Be careful though, because various soil deficiencies, sun damage, frost damage, cold damage and lack of water can produce the same symptoms as diseases.

If you are not sure what is attacking your plant, be on the safe side and clip off the sick parts. Throw them in the garbage — never compost anything that looks ill or bug-ridden.

Overwatering can spread several fungal diseases, identifiable by rotting stems and roots, stunted, sickly yellow plants or dark round spots on leaves that eventually dry up and drop, leaving holes in the leaves. If this is happening to your plants, ease up on watering or improve drainage in your pots.

Disease prevention includes ensuring good air circulation around your plants, proper watering, not touching wet plants (you could be moving spores around) and keeping the plant area clean, especially of rotting vegetation.

Here are some remedies for specific diseases.

Blackspot

Blackspot is a fungus disease of roses which appears as a nasty black spot on a rose leaf. Try fungicidal spray. Usually the only thing that really works is to trim off and discard (but not in the composter) affected leaves the moment you see them.

Botrytis

This fungal disease, also known as gray mold, causes leaf shoots to wilt and buds to turn black. Again try an organic fungicide. A badly infected plant — one with rotten stems and roots — should be thrown into the garbage. To deter gray mold, avoid spraying foliage late in the day. Make sure there is adequate air circulation around your plants. We read in the November 1992 issue of *Organic Gardening* that John Sutton of the University of Guelph is developing a biological control: beneficial bacterial spores mixed with talc. It will be spread by bees — it clings to their legs and bodies and wipes off on your plants when the pollinating bees visit them.

Mildew

Mildew is usually a mild fungal disease, if you catch it soon enough. It appears during hot, damp airless weather as a gray-white powder on leaf surfaces. Tuberous begonias seem to be especially sensitive to mildew, especially if the weather is cold and rainy for long periods. Verbena is also prone to it. Mildew responds fairly well to organic fungicides, if you spray from the moment you see it until it is completely gone.

GENERAL-PURPOSE HOME REMEDIES
AGAINST INSECTS AND DISEASES

If a pest has slipped through the iron gates of your preventive measures, there are many good do-it-yourself pest remedies. We have collected some of our favorites together here.

Feeling aggressive? A large insect can simply be hand picked off the plants and either squished or dropped in a jar of soapy or hot water. If you are reluctant to touch it, place the open jar under the leaf and scrape or knock the bug into the water. Too close for comfort? Then, cut off the leaf, bug and all, and let it drop into a jar.

Small, slow insects such as aphids can be squashed between gloved fingers, unless you think you would enjoy murdering them bare-handed. We both balk at squishing large, soft-bodied insects, however — too yucky.

The gardener can also use various traps and barriers. A sticky trap, a piece of yellow paper or plastic covered with a non-hardening glue, is available in some garden centers. As noted elsewhere, a number of flying insects (aphids, whitefly, gnats) home in on the yellow glue card. When the card is filled with glued-on insects, put it in the garbage. Some insects prefer red, so try one of each color. Make your own with colored cardboard and a thin film of old motor oil.

Slugs and earwigs are attracted to saucers of flat beer.

Some gardeners set out inverted grapefruit rinds, wedged slightly open on one side, near container plants. Both earwigs and slugs, night-time feeders, will crawl inside and sleep off their gluttonizing. Earwigs, which like close, dark places, can also be trapped in crinkled-up or rolled-up newspapers, slightly opened matchboxes, inverted flower pots, that sort of thing. Empty these traps every day, into a pail or jar of hot or soapy water, or throw them in a plastic bag and then into the garbage. Squish the bag if you want to be really sure they are dead. Do not forget to empty the traps, because the insects will simply wander out the next night in search of a free meal.

Balcony people might have to deal with cockroaches. We hear from an entomologist, who ought to know, that they are repelled by dried cucumber peels or can be drowned in a saucer of beer.

The desperate gardener can make some home-made sprays in the blender. You have your choice of ingredients. A purée of garlic, onion and/or hot pepper mixed into water, strained (put the solids in the compost), then sprayed on plants will reduce the attack of sucking insects such as mites and aphids. Hot pepper sprays can also be used to prevent mildew, as well as on plants infected, in the early stages, with leaf spot, rust and spore diseases. Never get this stuff in your eyes.

Onions on their own, puréed with water and then strained, can be used as a fungicide and a repellent for aphids. As well, one part dishsoap dissolved in 40 parts water controls many insects, including aphids, whitefly, leaf miners and spider mites.

If you do not want to mix up anything special, try blasting infected plants with a forceful spray from the garden hose to unseat these tiny marauders. But be aware that sometimes they jump right back on as soon as your back is turned.

If you feel particularly lazy, buy a commercial non-toxic soap spray, such as Safer's Insecticidal Soap, often found in garden centers.

When using any of these sprays, be sure to coat every part of the plant, the stem and undersides of the leaves, everywhere. Contact sprays work only if they hit the insect directly. After spraying, check in a week to see if any of the pests have returned. Many of these insects not only have very short reproductive cycles but their eggs are also usually not affected by the spray. It is best to spray in two-week cycles until you are sure all insects have been killed.

TEA TIME

Fungal diseases bothering you? Gray fuzz everywhere? Two shovelsful of compost soaked in a bucket of water for a week, then strained, give you compost tea, which is said to keep down fungal diseases. Water with it now and then, and wet down the leaves with the tea three or four times during the summer.

NOT QUITE NUCLEAR

A number of toxic biological sprays, composed of such substances as rotenone, ryania, pyrethrum and nicotine are available. They are not as harmful to the environment as the synthetic chemicals used in many commercial insecticides, but they should not be used indiscriminately. Because they are nerve toxins, they can kill beneficial as well as harmful insects. Some can make humans feel ill after exposure. The synthetic pyrethrums on the market are not biodegradable, so do not use them. Your authors do not recommend these sprays or other common garden poisons in your container gardens. You are living in close proximity to your plants, especially if you are sharing a small balcony with them. You do not want to sit out there inhaling poisons. We know we are being a bit of a bore about this, but we feel very strongly about it.

NOT A BUG, NOT A DISEASE,
BUT STILL A NUISANCE . . . WEEDS

Many people put a lot of effort into identifying weeds, but we would like to ask them just one question: why? No matter what its name, if we did not invite it to our party, it cannot attend. Anything alien is immediately pulled out of the pot, because weeds take precious water and nutrients away from the plant. This can stress the plant if enough weeds are present. The weed has a primitive, strong drive to survive and will not allocate resources on a fair basis.

It is important to pull weeds before they produce seeds,

otherwise the seeds will sprout where you do not want them. If you see a weed in flower, pull it out right away, because seeds will be the next step.

Weeds that lodge their tiresome selves between the stones of a patio are a particular drag, but a jab with the edge of a spade or trowel will dislodge them, or you can pull them by hand. Since they are growing in a tiny amount of soil they usually come out easily. A dribble of boiling water does wonders, but be careful to scald just the weed, not yourself. Also, do this only in warm weather, as in cold weather the temperature differential might crack stone. The boiling-water remedy is only appropriate for paving stones; using it anywhere else would kill off not only desirable plants but also beneficial soil micro-organisms.

We absolutely discourage using herbicides anywhere, but especially in a small space such as a patio, deck, porch or balcony. In these small spaces, it is like using an elephant gun to shoot an ant. Also, in these no-garden areas, humans are that much more likely to be close to these harmful compounds — the risk of side effects is too high. Just hand weed.

MORE NUISANCES . . .

Nematodes

An underground pest is the nematode, a microscopic worm. It is usually present in infected plant soil and difficult to eradicate without using poisonous chemicals. It is a root eater whose damage eventually can cause the plant to wither and collapse. It is best, if you suspect nematodes, to throw the plant out, along with its soil — not in the composter, needless to say. Scrub the pot out well before using it again.

Pigeons

Pigeons are balcony pests who might nip a plant or two in addition to fouling the places they sit. There have been many ingenious solutions to prevent pigeons from roosting, from dangling pie tins to plastic owls. One beleaguered balcony owner encased his entire area in chicken wire and grew his plants in this cage. Use your imagination. Cats tend to fall off balconies and so are not a good solution here.

Plant Thieves

Yes, plant pests can appear on two legs. Some are ordinary vandals and just feel like smashing your pots for the thrill of it. Some two-legged pests actually take the plants, pots and all, away. For three years running, one of your authors had a pot of purple passion vine stolen, no matter how she hid it in her porch plant display. Finally, it stopped — did the plant thief have enough finally to fill his or her window sill? Another neighbor, who loves to group geraniums in a half-barrel near her porch, was dismayed one morning to discover that three of the geraniums had been dug up and taken away. We cannot figure out how to bury mousetraps so they will work, and guard dogs seem a bit extreme. Even public gardens lose thousands of dollars worth of plant material to thieves every year. Wherever this happens, our local public garden places signs saying "plant stolen" — you never saw so many signs. Solutions, anyone?

Pollution

Another source of plant damage, high air pollution levels can cause yellowing, spotted or dropped leaves, distorted growth and general weakness. Keep your plants clean — wash off soot and dust. Nothing, except public pressure and action, will help clean up the air we and our plants breathe. Do your part.

Squirrels

Squirrels can be real pests as the summer season draws to a close. Driven by self-preservation, they begin collecting and burying food for the future. Squirrels often pick handy plant containers for this purpose. We have had pots of geraniums uprooted and window box displays decimated by energetic food-gathering squirrels. Having cats around (three each) has helped, although a squirrel sometimes slips through this guard and we have to replant a pot from time to time.

Chapter 16

No Nasty Surprises:

Safety Tips for Container Gardening

....

THE INFLEXIBLE GARDENER

Are you getting younger and more spry with every passing year? We certainly are not, and it makes us increasingly conscious of all the things that can be done to keep on gardening full tilt. If you find yourself pregnant or in a cast during gardening seasoning, you might want to try some of these ideas, too.

There is no law that says hanging plants have to be head-high. Lifting a full watering pot can be murder on arms, shoulders, backs. So fiddle with the height of a hanging basket so that it can be watered and weeded without your having to stretch. If you are really fond of head-high baskets, rig up a rope and cleat so they can be lowered for easier watering. For a diagram of how this works, see the material on hanging baskets in Chapter 8.

Would wheeled trolleys (see "Casters" in Chapter 4) beneath your larger planters help you arrange them for a party or trundle them into the garage for winter storage?

One of the simplest display solutions is to use a big solid outdoor table. A cedar or redwood picnic table is a good candidate. A narrow one lessens the stretching needed to reach the middle. Set planters on the picnic table's benches, if that degree of bending over does not strain you. Chapter 4 presents other ideas for raising planters to where they can be more easily reached.

Wearing a hat against the sun is only sensible, and so is sitting down for a brief rest now and then. High-seated chairs are easier for the elderly and the pregnant to get in and out of, although finding them might take a little hunting — outdoor chairs tend to be low-slung. Remember that wooden blocks (2–3 in./5–8 cm is often about right) can be nailed to the feet of standard-height plastic or wooden chairs.

SAFETY ON BALCONIES, PORCHES, AND RAISED DECKS

Insurance companies will tell you that the home is the most dangerous work site of all, so make sure your home play site is as safe as can be. It would be impossible to write an exhaustive list, so we ask you to keep safety always in mind. One nasty accident can ruin your whole day.

A SAFETY CHECKLIST:

- Good stout railings are essential. Check your local building code and by-laws to see how high off the ground a deck must be before railings are required. Ensure that posts are close enough so that pets and children cannot get caught or slip between them. The higher off the ground you are, the more important this is. Most railings are sensibly built, but if the people who had the house before you skimped, remedy this by retrofitting some posts. The commonly accepted rule of thumb for babycrib rails will serve well: you should be able to fit no more than three fingers, side by side, between the rails. There are laws about this sort of thing, and they change from time to time, so, again, check the building code and local by-laws.

- People with poor eyesight can manage staircases better if steps and railings are painted to contrast sharply with the rest of the deck or porch. Similarly, mark any change in level with a stripe of bright paint or an embedded strip of contrasting paving material.

- If you are setting out lines of potted plants to create a space within a space, do so only with tall plants. Short ones in unexpected places are just asking for someone to trip over them.

- Any deck railing that has a flat top wide enough for people to set down potted plants, glasses or plates should have a gallery, that is, a back railing that will stop things from falling down onto people passing below.

- If your balcony has a solid concrete railing, check it frequently to make sure it is still sound. One of us once lived next to — not in, thankfully — a building with questionable concrete construction. Inspectors tried to drill core samples for testing, but the concrete crumbled to sand as soon as the drill bits touched it. The moral is that concrete is not necessarily as strong and reliable as we would like to think.

- If you plan to hang window boxes on a balcony railing, hang them on the inside. This uses up precious space, but is better than having the box land on someone's head . . . maybe yours, even.

- If your porch or deck is reached with steps, you will want to set containers of flowers on them. Lovely, but advisable only if the steps are wide enough to accommodate both pots and stair users, including people bumping a baby buggy or shopping cart up and down them. If the steps are high, resist the temptation to put containers on more than the bottom three or four steps — any higher and they could become dangerous projectiles. If anyone using the steps is at all unsteady on their feet and needs a railing to hang on to, consider abandoning the flowers-on-steps idea completely.

- If hanging baskets are a part of your display, take a good look at what you plan to suspend them from — will the site support heavy pots? Put hooks into solid wood using long, stout screws or go to the hardware store and get the clerk to explain toggle bolts to you.

- If you have a balcony and pets, be extremely vigilant about keeping the door to the balcony shut. We have seen balconies enclosed by various elaborate wire mesh cages, but we have our doubts that they are completely safe. As well, balconies and unattended pets and children do not mix — even with cages. We cannot begin to imagine a mesh cage strong enough to keep in a child.

Chapter 17

Down to Specifics:

Special Considerations for Your Balcony, Deck, Patio, and Porch

....

Decks and patios resemble each other quite a bit, but not entirely. Porches and balconies have their similarities too. Below, we have assembled some points to ponder for each type of space.

DECKS

Decks are a subspecies of patio, the major difference being that decks are made of wood, patios are not. Also, it is quite easy and inexpensive to build a deck on two or more levels. Do-it-yourselfers can buy deck kits in many configurations at the larger lumber stores.

- The underneath of a raised deck presents problems, but not insoluble ones. If the deck is sufficiently high so that people can walk comfortably underneath it, there are two options: hard-surface the ground underneath and use it as a patio or leave the earth in place and create a low-light flowerbed. If it is not high enough to walk under, cover the gap between the ground and the deck's floor with lattice and treat it the same way as the gap between the ground and a porch floor (see below).

- Some decks come with built-in planters, which we are not so keen on. What if the previous owner did not do such a great job siting them? Or what if his idea of where they should go simply does not jibe with yours? So, if you are thinking of building a deck from scratch, opt for nonpermanent containers.

- If the wood decking under your planters is always wet, it will rot. There is, too, the possibility of mineral salts leaching out of pots and staining the wood. Arrange planters so that air circulates beneath them. Setting them on a trio of bricks works well.

- Wooden decks are raised above the ground by at least a few inches and so are cooler than masonry patios or concrete balconies. This makes decks easier to grow things on, since many plants do not like to be too hot.

- If your deck is large and low to the ground (under 18 in./45 cm), take a look at its underneath structure and see if it is a good candidate for retro-fitting some planting holes. Because this will involve cutting through the decking, the resulting edges will have to be supported, usually by adding joists.

- If your deck is more than 6–12 in./15–30 cm off the ground, install a railing for safety. There are by-laws to cover this sort of thing, so check them before committing yourself to anything. If municipal authorities do not like what you have done, they can make you change it.

PATIOS

Patios began their long, honorable history in ancient times as courtyards — flower, water and herb-filled retreats from the dust and noise of the outside world. In modern-day North America a patio has become any paved area near or adjacent to a house, yet their use as retreats from the world still holds.

- Patios made of stone or concrete absorb (and therefore throw back) a lot of heat. Thus, be sure the flow of air is not obstructed by too many fences, free-standing trellises or screens.

- If your patio is made of individual paving stones, try this charming design option: remove alternate stones and use them as growing spaces. One of us removed three stones from her patio and put a single rose bush in each. Looks great. This practice will, of course, cut down on the space available for tables and chairs. Since you will be planting in the ground, rather than in a container, you can use perennials and shrubs (see Appendix I).

- Weeds between paving stones are a perpetual nuisance. See Chapter 15 for nonchemical solutions.

- Trouble with a too-damp basement? Check the slope of your patio. Well-made ones are sloped slightly to carry water away from the house, but a poorly made one might do just the reverse.

- Define the edge of a patio with window boxes or other nicely arranged planters.

BALCONIES

Are you a mad keen gardener who through some hideous twist of fate is stuck with only a balcony on which to pursue your passion? If so, do not despair — meticulously tend as many plants as is physically possible. Choose persnickety plants that need a lot of attention. What you lack in quantity can be made up for in quality and obsessive behavior.

Some of us try to view long, narrow balconies as modern-day porches. Unfortunately, no one is likely to stroll by and stop for a chat, but that need not stop you from developing your balcony into an outdoor retreat. There are, however, a few problems to think about.

- Please read Chapter 17 on safety. Both of us hate heights and get the willies just thinking how far down it is off a balcony.

- Weight is a constant worry for many of us, gardeners and nongardeners alike. However, switch from thinking about personal pounds and kilograms and think about the weight of your soil-filled containers. A densely planted balcony will bear a considerable weight — one cubic foot/30 x 30 x 30 cm of dirt weighs anywhere from 50 to 90 lb./23 to 40 kg, so if you add up the volume of a few good-sized planters, you can see that the weight rises to half a ton or more in no time at all. What to do if you still want a big flower show? Refer to our material on potting mixes for advice on lightweight soil substitutes (Chapter 7).

• That damned back wall. It is so big, but the super would have a conniption fit if anything was attached to it. Read Chapter 4 for plant display strategies. Remember that plants growing close to a masonry wall will be subject to more heat than anywhere else on the balcony.

• Tired of carrying cans of water out to the balcony? Look for a special attachment that enables you to screw a regular garden hose to your kitchen tap. You will also need, for the other end of the hose, a small sprayer gun that can be turned on and off. Balcony hoses are not as much fun as garden hoses, because you cannot go around blasting everything in sight. (As everyone knows, half the point of gardening is that grownups get to play in the mud and water.) And we absolutely forbid you to blast that idiot from 4B (the one who plays heavy metal music at 120 decibels) as he walks past below.

• Wind is usually a problem on balconies — it dries out plants and, infuriatingly, tries to whip all their petals off. If you plan to use a screen, choose an openwork barrier, because a solid barrier creates more wind turbulence than it blocks. Even if that turbulence does not disturb your plants, it will rock the screen around and loosen it from its moorings and send it flapping through the neighborhood.

- If you like the trellis idea, arrange several so that they transform your balcony into a completely enclosed, perfectly private outdoor room.

- Set your pots in big deep saucers — you do not want water dribbling down to the neighbors below. Good Saucers Make Good Neighbors.

- Balconies experience different weather conditions than what occurs at ground level. The weather becomes more extreme the higher up you go. This is especially true in spring and autumn. If you have a sheltered, sun-catching balcony, you might be able to plant out earlier in the spring than other people, but watch out for low overnight temperatures way up there in the sky. If you like to get a head start, early planting out is permitted if you protect your plants on nights that threaten to plunge below freezing (remember, ground level's just-above-freezing will be your just-below-freezing point). Protection need not be elaborate — old bedsheets are fine. Spread them out in the evening and remember to remove them if daytime temperatures go more than a few degrees above the freezing point. You can do the same thing in autumn to stretch out blossoming as long as possible. If you do not have too many plants, move them indoors for the night and out again during a warm day.

- If your balcony faces north and does not get much direct sunlight, try low-light and foliage plants. Shiny white painted walls will make the most of any light that manages to sneak in. Since the super probably will not let you paint the balcony walls, paint plywood panels and lean them against the walls. Fasten or wedge them solidly into place so the wind does not shift them.

- East-facing balconies will get no more than four hours of sun. Try low-light plants or ones grown for their foliage.

- A west-facing balcony gets six or more hours of sunlight a day. This will support most high-light plants. Watch for too much heat.

- A south-facing balcony catches sunlight most of the day. Protect against excessive heat. Cool-loving plants such as lettuce and sweet peas are out. Heat-lovers such as portulaca, zinnia and geranium are in.

PORCHES

Porches are making an architectural comeback these days. We think it is high time — there is nothing like sitting out and watching the neighborhood go by. Mind you, these days the neighborhood tends to drive by instead of stroll by. Still, there are enough dog-walkers, baby-airers and milk-fetchers that sitting out front will result in one or two new acquaintances — always worth making in an increasingly impersonal world.

One of us has an absolutely wonderful porch on three sides of a big old house and the other is stuck out in the 'burbs in a bungalow, consumed with envy over this porch. If you, too, have porch-envy, consider building the porch of your dreams. Have it designed by an architect, because this job needs building permits and all sorts of things. This option will, of course, be limited by budget. Also, roof lines can limit your porch fantasies, because not all roof lines can be appropriately extended to become a porch roof. (In our book an unroofed porch is a deck, very nice in its own way, but still not a porch.)

- A porch is shady — half its appeal. So place shade-loving plants up against the house wall and sun-lovers on the outside edges of the porch — maybe hang window boxes from the railing.

- If you have an absolutely dreadful porch, you can always grow a big, vigorous vine over it. Virginia creeper or Boston ivy will cover the entire eyesore. This supposes that the porch is structurally sound — unsound porches must be repaired or removed, not burdened with heavy vines.

- Porches tend to be magnets for baby buggies, bicycles, roller skates, trowels, sneakers, you name it. No solution for this except major threats to the litterers or, better yet, installing an alternative storage place that is both convenient and out of sight. Although it might not be easy to get to, you can create a storage space underneath most porches. Box the lower portion in with lattice sheets and rig up a door so you can slither in and drag out seldom-used items. Remember that it will be damp, so put rustables in the garage, shed or basement.

- Porches need to be painted now and then, so perhaps

growing a rambling rose directly over it is not the brightest idea, unless you are into once-every-five-years masochism. There is a solution if you want to decorate your porch with a perennial vine or climber. Make or buy an extra-strong trellis of appropriate size; 1x2 unfinished cedar or redwood lath is best. Screw — don't nail — this trellis firmly to the supporting members of your porch. Now plant the perennial vine. It must be rooted in the ground, not a pot (see Appendix I). As it

MOBILE HOMES

Privacy can be a problem for those living in mobile homes who do not have the option of planting a hedge or building a fence. The solution is to plant a potted hedge.

Buy enough containers to stand shoulder to shoulder along the stretch you wish to "hedge." The containers should have a top diameter of about 12–15 in./30–40 cm, and a height about the same. Plant them with annuals that grow about 24–36 in./60–90 cm tall. Good choices are branchy, upright plants such as kochia (foliage only, turns red in autumn) or tall zinnias and marigolds. This will not, of course, create a real privacy hedge, but you will be surprised how much more private it makes you feel to have this barrier between you and the rest of the world.

Another problem with trailers is what to do about the wheel gap — the open space between the ground and the floor of the trailer. Even if you cover it with trellis, it is not a thing of beauty. An easy solution is to set a row of planters in front of it.

Take a look at your windows. Can brackets be installed for window boxes? Be sure the box's weight will not rip off the trailer's siding.

grows, keep a careful eye on it and make sure that it twines itself only around the trellis, not around the posts or any other permanent part of the porch. Now, when it comes time to paint the porch, simply detach the trellis from the posts, lay the whole thing, trellis and still-entwined plant, gently on the ground, and paint. You will find more detailed directions in Chapter 4.

Chapter 18

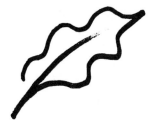

Take a Seat:

Outdoor Furniture

....

Furniture will be a large expense, so think carefully before buying. Decide whether you want wood, plastic, metal or rattan and which pieces will serve your purposes. Do not forget that to prolong the lifespan of chairs, tables and planters, store them indoors all winter long.

WHAT SHOULD IT BE MADE OF?

Plastic

We are fortunate that good-quality plastic furniture has recently become available at reasonable prices and in interesting shapes. If you buy only white, new purchases will always fit in with your old pieces.

Wood

Wood has a certain substance and attractiveness that is hard to beat. We are completely charmed by those big wide-armed Adirondack (Muskoka) chairs that are so inviting and comfortable. Mind you, wood is heavy, so if you enjoy constantly rearranging the furniture, or dragging it around to catch the sun, wood might not be the best choice.

Once you stain or paint any wood, you are committed to frequent refinishing. If the thought of this makes your eyes roll backwards, as it does ours, think about cedar and redwood. Unfinished cedar or redwood are naturally rot-resistant and low-maintenance — if left untreated, they will weather over the years to a most attractive silvery-gray.

We know that various types of preservative-treated lumber are available, but we are nervous about the chemicals. Whether the lumber is pressure-treated with toxic chemicals or the stuff is just painted on makes no difference. Pentachlorophenol (penta, for short) is a clear, effective preservative, but it is known to be toxic and is seldom used on lumber sold to home handypersons. The green-tinted preservative seen everywhere is sometimes copper naphthenate, but more often these days it is chromated copper arsenate (CCA). Treated lumber is usually accompanied by health warnings: wear eye protection and a breathing filter when working with it; never burn it (for fear of inhaling the smoke); never ingest any sawdust; sweep up carefully when done; wash skin and clothing thoroughly. To us, this sounds like fearsome stuff and is why we recommend unfinished redwood and cedar.

Metal

Metal usually means cast or wrought iron or, increasingly these days, cast aluminum. It also usually means those curlicued Victorian-looking pieces. Once painted, iron and aluminum look exactly the same, but of course the aluminum weighs much less. A small stone-paved area with a pleasant grouping of fancy white furniture in the middle is a beautiful classic. Set a pot of brilliantly colored geraniums (sun) or impatiens (shade) in the middle of the table and you are really in business.

However. Iron rusts. Rust-inhibiting paint is available in white and colors these days, which is a great boon. Iron furniture showing even a little bit of rust must be painted right away, or there will be big trouble. Chipped spots on aluminum furniture should be painted, too — you can get the right kind of paint at the hardware store.

Wicker/Cane/Rattan

We lust after the wicker, cane and rattan furniture we see in the glossy house-and-garden magazines, especially the chairs and sofas with huge comfortable chintz-covered cushions. However, our budgets do not stretch that far and our common sense does — these are not robust, all-weather or child-friendly materials. Granted, they are lightweight and so can be moved easily, but a high wind can send them wheeling away down the street or into a window, or into the arms of a low-down dirty rotten thief. Also, the pieces must be protected from rain — they quickly deteriorate and begin to rot if alternately soaked then dried in the sun. Squirrels love to gnaw on them and cats sharpen their claws on the mesh.

As we write, we are beginning to hear reports about wicker that can safely be left out in all weathers, but even if this is true, wind-borne grit, dirt and city pollution will still have to be washed or vacuumed out of all those crevices. Now you see why plastic is so popular.

WHAT PIECES TO BUY?

Choose pieces that complement the theme and scale of your garden room. Do you want comfort above looks? Is the furniture well made? Check that joins are sturdy and upholstery is fade-resistant. Is it easy to clean? To store? If the piece is the latest trendy offering, wait two years — the price will drop by half.

Tables

Glass tabletops should be tempered. If extreme wind is predicted, take it indoors lest something heavy fall on it. Our neighbor's chimney blew down in a high wind and covered the backyard with bricks.

Plastic tabletops are soft and prone to scratches. Even small scratches catch dirt. One of us has a small plastic outdoor table with a molded basket-weave finish — a curse, since all the passing grit catches in it. The wretched thing always looks grubby, no matter how much it is scrubbed.

We are fond of those heavy wooden picnic tables with

attached benches. They make a great surface for dirty work, such as potting up, which would scratch and stain plastic, metal or glass-topped tables. Despite their having fallen from favor lately, they are still easy to find. Be warned: they usually need to be assembled. Pine is cheap, but does not perform especially well and must be refinished frequently. Instead choose cedar or redwood. A sheet makes an excellent tablecloth that can be thumb-tacked in place if you forget to buy a set of those little clips.

Consider buying two tables — one to be left in place all summer, plus a collapsible one to be brought out for extra company.

Chairs

One chair per family member plus a few extra for guests will be sufficient. Stacking chairs make the most of smaller spaces. Do you want separate dining chairs and easy chairs, or can you find ones that will serve both purposes? Easy chairs with adjustable backs are extremely comfortable. Always try a chair on for size before buying, since chair-fit is a personal thing.

We like chairs with ample cotton-covered cushions. Sitting on uncovered wire mesh or wood is hard on the unpadded posterior. Equally, we do not enjoy sticking to plastic-covered cushions that peel off a layer of flesh when we struggle out of their sweaty embrace.

However, there is a price to pay for cotton cushions. If you have cats, or the neighbors do, you will have to cover the cushions or bring them in when not in use. If not, before you know it there will be sleepy gatherings of the neighborhood cats, who will graciously leave matts of hair behind as a thank you for the comfortable nap.

Loungers

These are expensive and not everyone sunbathes as much as they used to, so make sure they will be used. Among the several styles available, the most versatile have adjustable backs and foot rests. Wheeled models are especially easy to move around.

Benches

We cannot for the life of us imagine why it has taken so long for park bench type seating to hit the stores. There are many styles now available on a widely sliding price scale — teak, anyone?

A variation on the bench is the swing-seat. It can be bought with its own frame, which avoids in-ground installation. Do you want to make your highrise balcony look like an old-fashioned porch? This is just the thing, although you might have to do some searching to find a really nice one.

Appendix I

The Container Garden Battle:

Jack Frost vs. Perennials, Shrubs, Trees and Roses

....

We have referred several times throughout the book to this section on frost and the container gardener, because we want to emphasize that any containerized plant will die if it is left outdoors during winters in which below-freezing temperatures are the norm.

Perennial plants and shrubs growing in a regular flowerbed are insulated from extremes of cold by the surrounding earth mass, which is of course enormous. They are further insulated by the snow. This all means that they go dormant in early winter and stay that way until spring. Now, a container-grown perennial plant or shrub that is sitting out on your deck, patio, porch or balcony all on its lonesome in the middle of winter is exposed to the elements from all sides. No insulation at all. What happens to it as it sits out there shivering? The dreaded freeze-thaw cycle, that's what.

Suppose there is a sunny day in the midst of a January thaw. The sun's rays can hit the potted, uninsulated root mass and thaw it through completely, since there is so little insulating earth present. This makes the plant rise slightly inside its pot, enough to rip off the tiny little root hairs. To makes matters worse, when night comes and the temperature drops, the whole thing freezes again and sinks back, ripping off more root hairs. This can happen over and over, and is called the freeze-thaw cycle. Why is it such a disaster to lose those root hairs? They are the most active part of the root when it comes to feeding the plant, so when spring arrives the plant cannot feed itself adequately and, of course, dies.

There is no point in planting perennials in pots and treating them as annuals, throwing them into the composter come the first frost. Just-purchased perennials are sad little things, unlikely to flower much that first year. Perennials need two years in the bed before they look the way they do in the pictures.

The same goes for shrubs and trees — apart from the fact that they are too expensive to treat this way. The photographs of luscious patios with olive trees growing in big tubs were all taken in warm climates such as southern California, the south of France, Greece, places like that, populated by people who think that if they have to wear a sweater in the middle of January they are having a bad winter. However. We offer you an idea for rose-growing. Keep reading.

ABOVE-GROUND ROSES

We know you are dying to grow potted roses on your deck, patio, balcony, porch, anywhere you can fit in a container. So are we. There is something about roses that makes everyone's eyes grow round with desire. Unfortunately, potted roses and below-freezing winters do not mix. What to do? Treat them as annuals. You can have a very nice display of roses if you are willing to buy new plants every year and throw them away when winter comes.

This is not as spendthrift as it might at first seem, because a potted rose will cost you about the same as one and a half big thick paperback novels by Stephen King or James Michener. You can use just one (rose, not novel) as the central focus for a very small space. Buy two scented ones and place them on each side of your favorite outdoor reading chair. Three can be placed to punctuate a long, narrow space. Four can be placed so they anchor the corners of a square space.

Potted roses (bare-root plants take too long to bring to bloom) on sale in spring are usually on the point of blossoming. They will bloom until June, take July off, then will blossom again in August, so you can enjoy about the same floral display as those who nurse their in-ground roses through the years.

Save yourself some aggravation and wait to buy roses until it is warm enough to put them outside right away — wait for the last frost date for your area. In much of Canada, this means Victoria Day weekend. Buy from a good nursery, which costs a dollar or two more, but where you will find the best choice and the healthiest stock. Choose the plants that have the most flower buds showing and are the most pleasing shape — bushy and symmetrical, without long whips that wander off into nowhere.

Once home, stand them in full sun, keep them evenly moist and fertilize lightly (half what the package says) every three weeks. Roses are prone to fungal diseases, so place them where they can catch mild breezes. Spray with an organic fungicide if their leaves sprout a grayish fuzz. Blackspot looks exactly the way it sounds. The best way to deal with black-spotted leaves is to clip them off and put them in the garbage (not the composter). Watering with compost tea — two shovelsful of compost soaked in a bucket of water for a week, then strained — is said to keep down fungal diseases, especially if you wet down the leaves with the tea once a month or so.

When frost arrives, put the leaves and soil in the composter and throw the rest away, because the tough woody parts will take forever to decompose.

There is one substantial advantage to the one-summer romance approach to rose growing: roses really prefer mild winters that only dip to a few degrees below freezing. Thus, in-ground growers must choose their varieties according to what is likely to survive their local winter. The harsher the winter, the more limited their selection. If you plan to chuck it out come winter anyhow, you can choose any rose you like.

However, having said that, we want to give you the following piece of good news. The much-loved tender roses — hybrid tea, grandiflora, floribunda, polyantha — are your best bet for the kind of use described here. Shrub roses, also called rugosa roses, are meant to grow quite large over time, and newly purchased ones need a couple of years of in-ground growth before they look like much.

AN EXCEPTION

The above advice does not, of course, apply to readers who might have a small strip near the deck or patio where they could plant a rose or two right in the living earth. In this case, the usual rules for growing perennial material should be followed. (If we may be so bold, we would like to suggest our first book, *The Reluctant Gardener*, which contains, ahem, much excellent advice for in-ground, cold-climate gardeners.)

CHRYSANTHEMUMS

The no-garden gardener can grow these long-lasting autumn favorites the same way as roses. Buy heavily budded plants when they are first offered for sale in early autumn, arrange them attractively in the outdoor room and enjoy them until frost does its nasty number. Then compost the whole plant and its soil. Many owner-operators of flowerbed-type gardens do the same thing, because chrysanthemums are fairly ordinary foliage plants all summer long, bursting into song only when autumn comes.

Appendix II

A Note to Plant Collectors:

....

We urge you not to smuggle in plants from foreign holiday locations to add to your container collections. You could inadvertently spread insects, plant diseases and viruses that could cause crippling damage to our agricultural, forest, nursery and fruit industries. The "hungry hitchhiker" frequently travels without its natural predators and, given the right conditions, little prevents its multiplication and the resulting horticultural havoc.

Nowadays, plant-importation restrictions are designed to prevent the importation of such things as hard-to-detect insect eggs hiding underneath leaves or invisible viral time-bombs lurking in plant tissues.

Agriculture Canada's Plant Protection Division was established to prevent such horticultural devastation and also to help Canadian plant importers. Any traveling gardener who wants to return laden with living souvenirs must plan ahead and begin the procedure before leaving Canada.

After deciding what plants you plan to collect, write the Permit Office, Plant Protection Division, Agriculture Canada, Ottawa, Ontario K1A 0C6, requesting an import permit. It is necessary to specify your destination and the plants by common name and botanical name (genus and species). As well, list the different ways you might be importing them: as seeds, seedlings, bare-rooted plants or rooted cuttings. In most cases, plants are not allowed in if they are growing in soil. The Office will then tell you if the plants are allowed in and are not on the endangered plant list, as well as the form in which they can be imported. At the point of entry into Canada, you must show the certificate and the plants. They may be inspected on site.

Appendix III

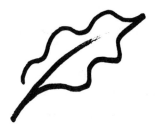

Selected Bibliography:

Allen, Oliver E., and the Editors of Time-Life Books, *The Time-Life Book of Shade Gardens*, Time-Life Books, New York, 1979.

Buckley, A.R., *Canadian Garden Perennials*, Hancock House, Saanichton, B.C., 1977.

Calkins, Carroll C., *Reader's Digest Illustrated Guide to Gardening in Canada*, Reader's Digest, Montreal, 1979.

Cullen, Mark, and Lorraine Johnson, *The Real Dirt: The Complete Guide to Backyard, Balcony and Apartment Composting*, Penguin, Markham, Ont., 1992.

Ettlinger, Steve, *The Complete Illustrated Guide to Everything Sold in Garden Centers (Except the Plants)*, Macmillan, New York, 1990.

Fell, Derek, *Essential Herbs*, Michael Friedman Publishing, New York, 1990.

Fell, Derek, *Garden Accents*, Michael Friedman Publishing, New York, 1987.

Franklin, Stuart, *Building a Healthy Lawn*, Storey Communications, Pownal, Vermont, 1988.

Ferguson, Nicola, *Right Plant, Right Place*, Pan Books, London, 1986.

Geiger, Maggy, *The Window Box Primer*, Popular Library, New York, 1979.

Hart, Rhonda Massingham, *Bugs, Slugs, and Other Thugs*, Storey Communications, Pownal, Vermont, 1991.

Horten, Alvin, ed., *Gardening in Containers*, Ortho, San Francisco, 1983.

Kramer, Jack, *Patio Gardening*, HP Books, Los Angeles, 1982.

Lima, Patrick, *The Harrowsmith Perennial Garden*, Camden House, Camden East, Ont., 1987.

Newcomb, Duane, *The Apartment Farmer . . .*, J.P. Tarcher, Los Angeles, 1976.

Osborne, Richard, ed., *Sunset Ideas for Hanging Gardens*, Lane Publishing, Menlo Park, Cal., 1974.

Osborne, Robert, *Roses for Canadian Gardens: A Practical Guide to Varieties and Techniques*, Key Porter Books, Toronto, 1991.

Shields, Dinah, and Edwinna von Baeyer, *The Reluctant Gardener: A Beginner's Guide to Gardening in Canada*, Random House, Toronto, 1992.

Shewchuk, George, *Rose Gardening on the Prairies*, University of Alberta, Edmonton, 1988.

Taylor's Guide to Water-Saving Gardening, Houghton Mifflin, Boston, 1990.

Wright, R.C.M., *The Complete Handbook of Plant Propagation*, Macmillan, New York, 1973.

Index

NOTES

NOTES